BINDON

BINDON

FIGHTER, GANGSTER, ACTOR, LOVER – THE TRUE STORY OF JOHN BINDON, A MODERN LEGEND

WENSLEY CLARKSON

JB
JOHN BLAKE

Published by John Blake Publishing Ltd,
3, Bramber Court, 2 Bramber Road,
London W14 9PB, England

www.blake.co.uk

First published in hardback in 2005

ISBN 1 84454 116 9

All rights reserved. No part of this publication may be reproduced, stored in a retrieval system, or in any form or by any means, without the prior permission in writing of the publisher, nor be otherwise circulated in any form of binding or cover other than that in which it is published and without a similar condition including this condition being imposed on the subsequent publisher.

British Library Cataloguing-in-Publication Data:

A catalogue record for this book is available from the British Library.

Design by www.envydesign.co.uk

Printed in Great Britain by CPD

3 5 7 9 10 8 6 4 2

© Text copyright Wensley Clarkson 2005

Papers used by John Blake Publishing are natural, recyclable products made from wood grown in sustainable forests. The manufacturing processes conform to the environmental regulations of the country of origin.

Every attempt has been made to contact the relevant copyright-holders, but some were unobtainable. We would be grateful if the appropriate people could contact us.

In Memory of John Bindon, Alan Stanton
and Mickey Bindon.

Author's Note

It is more than twenty years since I first moved into Fulham and heard about the legendary John Bindon. His name came up everywhere, from the dinner parties of South Kensington to the seediest riverside nightclubs. Now, many years of investigation in homes, pubs and clubs across west London have culminated in this biography. I don't know whether it'll be a bestseller, but I'm certain you'll be enthralled by the life of this outrageous character. It isn't just another book about a cold and dark criminal – there truly were many more sides to John Bindon.

Researching Bindon's life has left me with myriad impressions of the man himself, because his story is extremely complex. As I started to write it, I realised I had a great deal of material I couldn't use because the sources had shady, ulterior motives and my aim has always been to show Bindon in the light he truly deserved.

More importantly, as I researched this book, I realised that Bindon's own words summed him up best: 'I'm not scared. I've lived the life of ten men.'

The story you are about to read is the one John Bindon would have wanted to tell. It is a legend that has grown ever more fascinating since his death: this is the truth about a man who made an impression on everyone he met, from the lowest of the low to the most powerful family in this land.

In researching this book, I have been taken into the confidence of many people who, for their own reasons, would prefer to remain anonymous. I have respected the requests of these mysterious 'friends', and I need only say that my decision to do so is more to protect the guilty than the innocent.

Wensley Clarkson
London, 2005

Tributes to Bindon

Freddie Foreman (businessman)
Bindon's manor of Fulham, west London, had quite a reputation back in the old days. I used to go down there with a crew from Bermondsey and I soon heard about John Bindon. I've crossed swords with everyone from judges to government ministers to the meanest old bastards imaginable, but John Bindon was something special. He could be relied upon 100 per cent if you had a problem, and he thoroughly deserves to have a book written about him.

Clemmie Simon (*Vogue* model)
John and I were incredibly close and I needed him so badly. He saved me many times. He left me with so many good memories. It was a crazy time but I wouldn't be here today if it wasn't for him.

Joe Pyle (businessman)

Bindon was one of the hardest men in London. If the Twins had a problem, he was the man to sort it out. If you owned a bar or a nightclub and someone was being a nuisance then John was your man. He'd tell 'em to stay away or get hurt. Bindon also did some debt collecting and stuff like that for me. He was good like that. He wasn't greedy, never took the piss and could really handle himself. Bindon wasn't a hardened professional criminal like a lot of others. He wanted desperately to succeed in the film world and he was probably the first working-class kid I ever knew who broke into that exclusive club. We all admired him for making his name away from the underworld. God bless him!

Terry de Havilland (Chelsea shoe designer)

I first met John at my shop in the King's Road when it was buzzing round the clock with models, photographers and actors. Everyone gravitated to my gaff. The John Bindon I got to know was kind, warm-hearted and blessed with the biggest weapon any man could possess, which went down well with the ladies whatever their class or creed! John was comfortable in every social circle, from villains to the royals. He treated everyone the same and that was part of his extraordinary charm. He never put on an act. What you saw was what you got. What a character! What a life he led! It's all the quieter now without him.

Dana Gillespie (singer/actress)

John Bindon was like a big brother to me. He'd turn up at my house in South Kensington, sit himself down and enjoy a bloody good sing-song. It didn't matter who he met, he got

Chapter One

on famously with all of them. Within minutes of being introduced to Princess Margaret on Mustique, he had her in stitches. And when it came to rescuing damsels in distress, he was the king! Women flocked to him, and his skills in the bedroom were legendary. He loved all the attention, but he was fiercely loyal and I always knew that, if I had a problem, he was one of the few people I could go to for help.

Richard Cole (legendary tour manager)

Bindon was always good value. Led Zeppelin loved him, especially their crazy bastard of a drummer, John Bonham. Bindon was a madman in the nicest possible way. He wasn't scared of anyone and it showed. God help those who upset him, but he never hit anyone who didn't deserve it.

BINDON'S MANOR

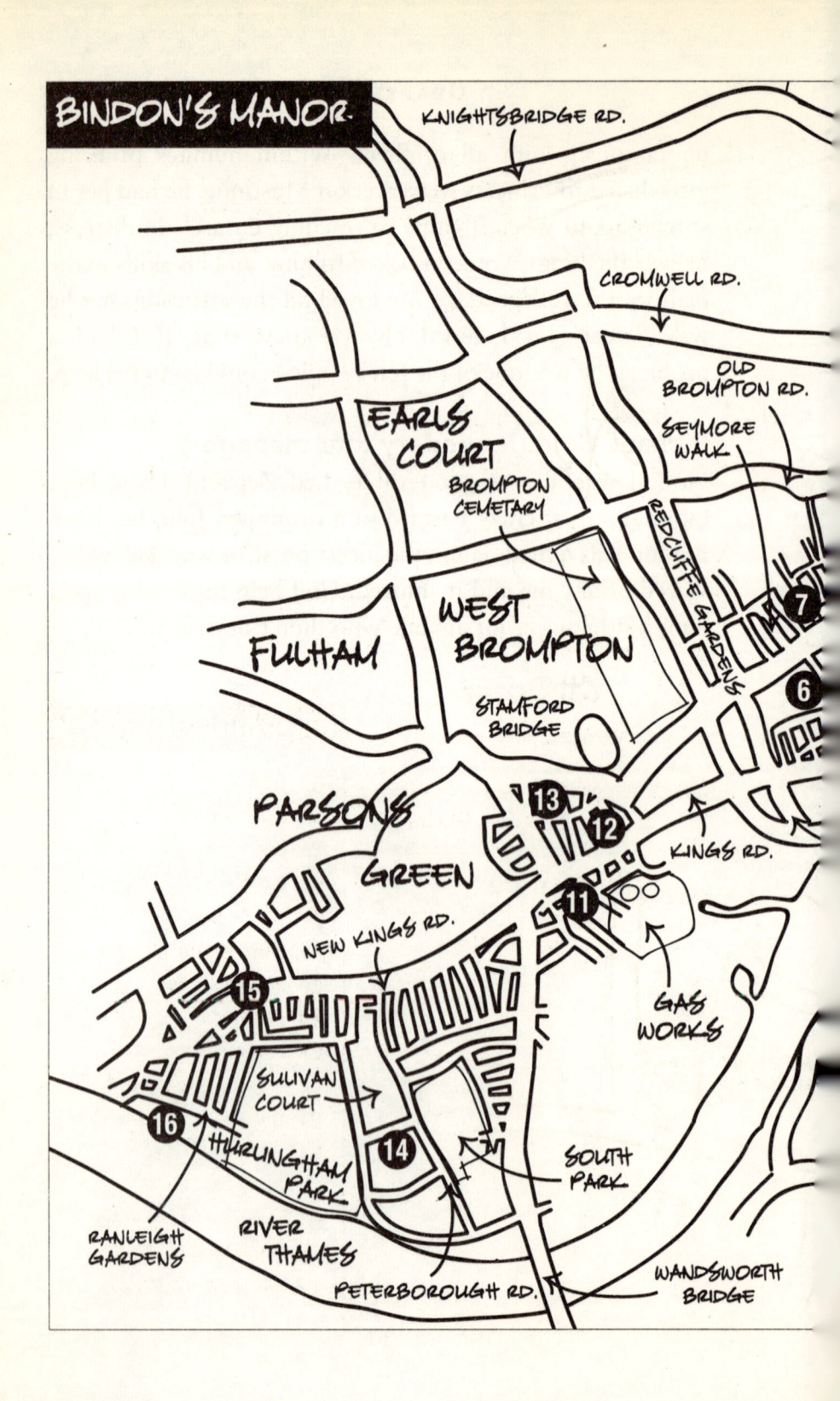

KEY

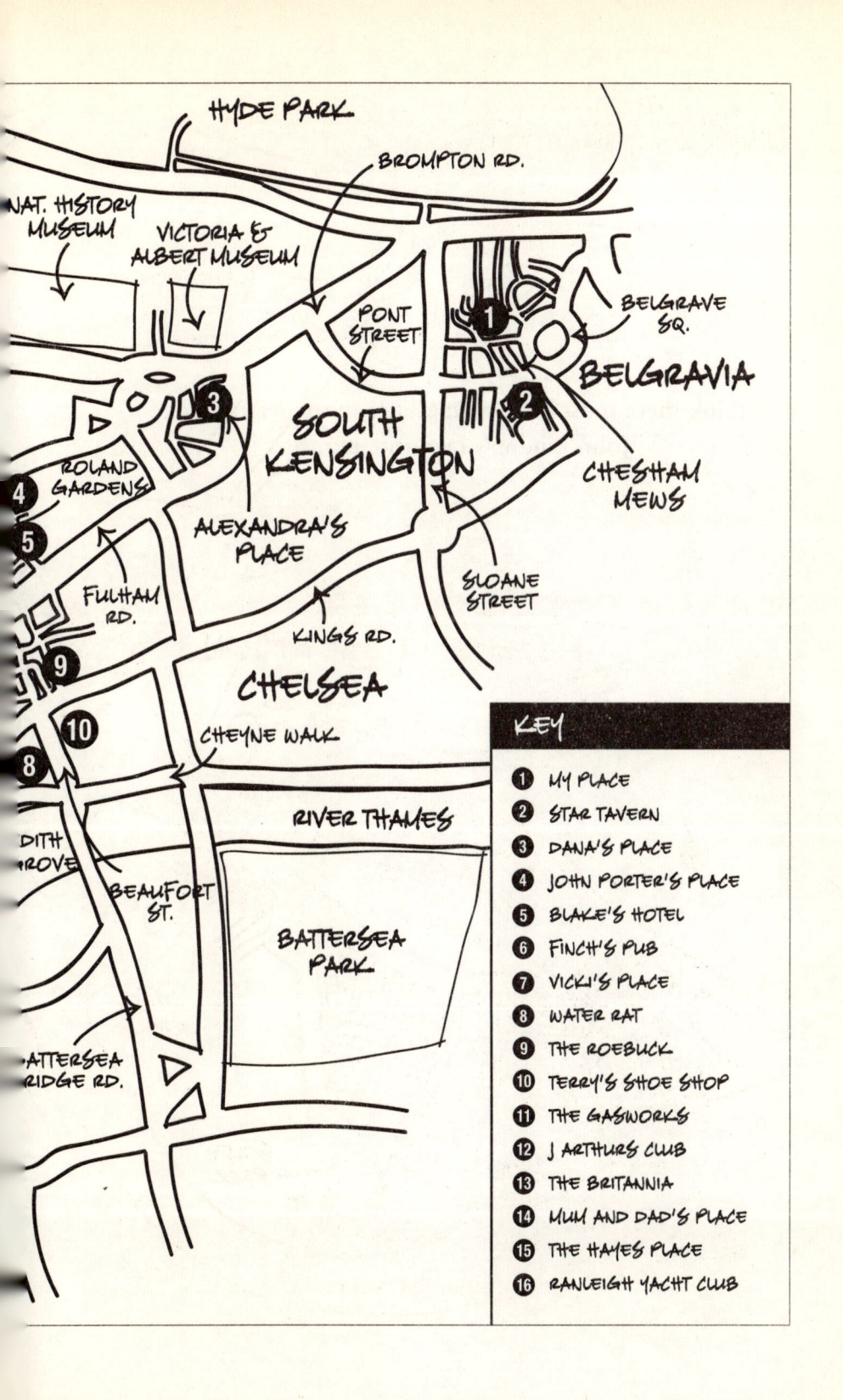

1. MY PLACE
2. STAR TAVERN
3. DANA'S PLACE
4. JOHN PORTER'S PLACE
5. BLAKE'S HOTEL
6. FINCH'S PUB
7. VICKI'S PLACE
8. WATER RAT
9. THE ROEBUCK
10. TERRY'S SHOE SHOP
11. THE GASWORKS
12. J ARTHURS CLUB
13. THE BRITANNIA
14. MUM AND DAD'S PLACE
15. THE HAYES PLACE
16. RANLEIGH YACHT CLUB

'I think there must have been a little misunderstanding.'
John Bindon's favourite phrase

Chapter One

Ned and Mary Monaghan always wanted the best for their eleven children, so it was only natural that, when they moved over from Ireland in the late 1920s to west London, Ned got himself a job – at Battersea Power Station overlooking the Thames – and started saving every penny he could manage. Ned was a tough character with a face as hard as granite and bright-blue piercing eyes that lit up when he had a pint of Guinness in front of him

By the time the eldest of his many children were in their late teens, Ned had saved up enough cash to buy a row of dilapidated workmen's cottages a mile up the Thames from Battersea in a quiet Fulham street near Wandsworth Bridge called Hugon Road. When daughter Cicely – known as Ciss to everyone – married a shy giant of a Cornish man called Dennis Bindon in the late 1930s, Ned gave the top half of 25 Hugon Road to the couple. It was a time of extreme hardship, so without Ned's help they might well have ended up in a workhouse somewhere along the river's edge. Ned and Mary were devout Catholics, so the only condition attached to Ciss and Dennis's new home was that they had to make the ten-minute walk each Sunday to attend the Holy Cross Catholic church at the back of nearby Hurlingham Park.

As Ciss's nephew Gordon Wilson said many years later, 'Old man Ned was bloody clever to buy those houses, but his main aim was to keep the family together. That's what it was like back then. You stuck to your own whatever the circumstances.'

'Monaghan Terrace', as Ned's houses were known, eventually became home to all eleven of his children and their respective families, and no one dared challenge the Monaghans. 'They were a polite, well-brought-up family, but if you crossed them you did so at your peril!' recalled one neighbour who still lives in Hugon Road to this day.

Three of Ciss's eight brothers, Tommy, Nobby and Jackie, were a fearsome bunch always on the lookout for their three sisters. 'They was good street fighters,' explained Gordon Wilson. 'Not in a villainous way, just in a way that if someone was rude to a woman then they'd offer them outside. On a Friday night those three brothers would give all challengers a right seeing-to if they asked for trouble. I don't think they ever lost a fight.' Jackie especially was renowned as an amateur boxer of great note in west London, and went more than thirty bouts without defeat.

Eventually all three brothers joined the merchant navy, as did Dennis Bindon, as an engineer, shortly after his

Chapter One

marriage to Ciss. 'They were attracted to the merchant navy because you weren't told what to do like you were in the services,' said Gordon, but following the outbreak of war in 1939 it proved in many ways a much riskier career. U-boats prowled the Atlantic looking for ships to sink, and often there was little or no cover for such convoys – Nobby Monaghan's ship was torpedoed, although he miraculously survived to tell the tale.

The only good news for Dennis and Ciss Bindon in the early days of the war was the birth in 1940 of their first child, a boy called Michael. However, Dennis only first met the boy on home leave nearly a year after he was born. Ciss was determined to have a big family because that was how she had been brought up, and John Arthur Bindon was born on 4 October 1943, nine months after another brief spell of home leave for Dennis. As the second son, little John might have expected to be relatively ignored, especially when his sister Geraldine turned up a few years after him; but Ciss had a soft spot for her middle child because he was always smiling and never seemed to cry much compared to his older brother.

Home for the Bindons remained the top half of that rundown terraced house bought by Ned Monaghan a few years earlier. Below them, another of Ciss's sisters was also bringing up her young family. By the time John was born, Germany's spread across Europe had already been stemmed, but the air raids on London continued. Many times baby John and brother Michael were woken by the sound of falling bombs as Ciss checked the blackout curtains and stayed close to her two sons until danger passed. Little John never forgot his mother's comforting hug. It was his security blanket. With Hitler's bombs targeting riverside factories and homes, there were still times when the sky was bright red from the fires burning through the night, people standing blankly on street corners with their homes reduced to piles of rubble. John Bindon later said that all this death and destruction taught him from an early age not to worry about money and possessions, because you never knew when it might all end.

The war-torn backstreets of west London were filled with shabby-looking characters shuffling around trying to scratch a living. Children roamed the streets in threadbare clothes while just a mile up the King's Road in Sloane Square the wealthy continued shopping at Peter Jones department store. Baby John was too young to be taken from his mother and evacuated to the countryside, so occasionally he was pushed in a makeshift pram – little more than a wooden box with wheels on it – up the King's Road to 'where the rich people lived'. He told a friend many years later that one of his first memories was entering a department store in Oxford Street to have his hair cut, a special treat for a youngster from a poor background.

Life was undoubtedly hard back then, although it all seemed full of fun to cheery little Johnny Bindon. The family might have struggled to put meat on the table for dinner, but there was an optimistic, uplifting Irish spirit about Ciss, and, since Dennis was away most of the time on the high seas, she was the driving force behind the family during those early days. The Bindons weren't exactly living in the most affluent part of town. Hugon Road was so close to the river that rats would pour through the back yard most nights and the noise of the

Chapter One

hooters of the tugs towing barges upriver often went on all through the evening and into the early hours. The Bindons even accepted hand-me-down clothes from some of the rich families in the big posh houses of nearby Chelsea and Belgravia for whom Ciss did the cleaning. But Ciss made sure that John and his brother Michael were always well fed and looked after, although, as a virtual single parent, she didn't always manage to keep tabs on the youngsters.

Behind the property in Hugon Road was an outhouse with a tiny kitchen and a bath and toilet. The kitchen area was for cooking, eating and keeping warm. Cheese and meat hung in the larder and the smells that wafted through the small house were a strange combination of bread and slightly off ham, a luxury bought from local spivs and kept for special occasions. Meals included potatoes three times a day and the occasional joint of beef or lamb if Dennis was back from overseas. A special treat would be apple pie or rhubarb crumble for pudding. Depending on the state of the finances, there would be fish and chips on Fridays.

Many years later, John Bindon agreed that no child could have asked for more love than he received from his mother. His father, on the other hand, was a harder, more distant character, although he never shirked his duty to ensure that Ciss was provided with the money to keep the family afloat. Back home in Hugon Road, little John – already clearly his mother's favourite – would sit on her knee as she bewitched him with glorious stories of her Irish heritage. Bindon said later that he adored listening to Ciss telling stories about Ireland before singing her heart out with her sister and other relatives at the sing-songs they held at home virtually every weekend. She would be surrounded by the other wives in their flowery pinafores and the men in their cloth caps and mufflers. Many of Bindon's young cousins would watch as Ciss and her sister entertained everyone.

But there were other memories which provide a definite clue as to why John Bindon took such an extraordinary course in life. He was just a toddler when he first encountered his father's detachedness. He had been sitting at the family's bare wooden kitchen table with a Formica top when Dennis Bindon arrived home from yet another long sea voyage. He was hungry and not very communicative, and, when little John asked his father if he had brought him a present from his travels, he yelled at the child to keep quiet. Bindon was so terrified he slid down underneath the table and sobbed. For the following few years, Bindon often cowered beneath that table when his father came into the kitchen: clearly Dennis's presence in the Bindon home provoked a change of atmosphere. As Bindon grew older, he started to understand the problematical relationship between Ciss and Dennis and how much pressure his father was under just to provide enough money for the family's weekly shopping bill. As one relative explained, 'Dennis wasn't a violent man but he was a very quiet, reserved individual, and that made him seem more stern than perhaps he really was.'

Dennis Bindon had a near obsession with crosswords, and would spend hours filling in *The Times* crossword. Dennis was also keen on games such as chess and draughts, and was an avid reader. It was only natural, therefore, that he should try to encourage his children to indulge in his passions. But John used to retreat from the sitting-room

Chapter One

area the moment he saw his father take out his glasses and begin studying the latest crossword puzzle in complete silence. 'You could say they weren't exactly close,' one of Bindon's oldest friends recalled. 'Dennis didn't like aggressive behaviour, and Mickey and Johnny could be aggressive little buggers at times, although it was usually in a very jovial way. They'd do things to each other to make the other one laugh, but they also fought like cat and dog. The old man used to say, "If you behave like an animal, I will treat you like an animal." That was his way of telling them to behave.'

Nevertheless, Michael and John often competed for their father's attention. Gordon Wilson explained that 'In those days many types of food were scarce and one day Ciss bought Dennis two cream cakes for his tea and cream cakes were things you didn't see very often back then. So Johnny, having a wicked sense of humour, removed a bit of the cream from one of the cakes and placed it on the corner of his mouth so, when Mickey came in, he saw it and said, "What have you done?" John immediately offered Mickey the other cake and said, "It's yours," so Mickey grabbed it and wolfed it down – at which point Johnny produced the other one and said, "You just ate Dad's tea." Mickey started crying in fear of what would happen, while Johnny was killing himself laughing. Then his dad walks in and he grasses Mickey up and tells Dennis he's eaten one of his cakes. Then Mickey tells his dad what really happened and Dennis says, "I'll tell you what I'm going to do, for being so devious." Then he took the other cake and gave it to Mickey and let him eat it as well, which made Johnny cry because Mickey ended up having both cakes.'

Practical jokes were soon little Johnny's stock-in-trade. On one occasion, Ciss and her sister were downstairs in Hugon Road when they heard a lot of banging and crashing. They went up to see what was happening. 'There's someone in the wardrobe, there's someone in the wardrobe,' screamed out one of Bindon's cousins. The others appeared to be under their bedclothes fast asleep. 'Go back to sleep and stop being so stupid,' said Ciss. But the child was insistent. Ciss threw open the wardrobe and there was Johnny on Michael's shoulders with Dennis's overcoat on and wearing a cheese-cutter cap. They were about seven foot tall and they screamed at Ciss who passed out with fright.

Ciss's role as organiser and disciplinarian at home meant she could sometimes be a hard taskmaster. 'There was a side to her you didn't mess with,' Gordon Wilson explained, 'but the other side of her would give you her last penny. She was so soft-hearted. One time, we pulled up at some traffic lights on Putney Bridge and she made us wait while she got out the back of the car and went over to a tramp sitting by a wall and gave him a few cigarettes. She would do anything for anyone who had a hard-luck story.'

A lot of John Bindon's young playmates' homes were destroyed by Hitler's bombs, and many ended up being housed in so-called prefab buildings on available wasteland in the area. Many of these plots sloped down to the River Thames on sites that, until a couple of years previously, had been rows of neat two-up two-down terraced cottages similar to the one in which the Bindons lived. John went into a friend's pre-fab and was impressed by what he saw: Bakelite and Formica fittings, fold-away ironing boards

Chapter One

and tables. They were warm and cosy and each property even had a plot of land, an asbestos shed and a mound of topsoil to make into a garden.

Sometimes John and Michael would sit on the precarious roof of the bombed-out factory at the end of nearby Distillery Lane with a mob of other tearaways and watch planes fly past to Heathrow Airport. The boys would wave up at the aircraft in the hope they would be spotted. Both brothers were soon raising extra cash by stealing empty glass bottles and taking them back to the local sweet shop for their deposits.

With the war well and truly over, life started looking up. One neighbour even bought a car, which he allowed all the local kids, including Michael and John, to sit in outside his house. And the boys were overjoyed when one of their uncles purchased a Ford motorcar and took them and their mother on a trip to Kensington High Street. They were awestruck by the big stores – C&A, Barkers, Derry and Toms – with their windows dressed and illuminated; then they saw Harrods, and men and women walking along Knightsbridge in fancy suits and £30 dresses. It was all a far and distant cry from downtrodden Fulham, just a couple of miles down the road.

On another occasion when John and Michael were out with their uncle, they drove along Piccadilly and spotted lots of well-dressed women in seamed stockings talking to soldiers and civvies on the pavement. John later recalled that all the women looked very pretty. Their uncle called them 'brasses', and it was only years later that the Bindon boys actually learned what that expression meant.

During another trip to the West End, the family made it as far as Soho where people of all colours and creeds seemed to pop out from anonymous doorways. They paid a visit to the cinema, whose wall-to-wall posters of Mickey Mouse, Donald Duck and Bugs Bunny caught their eyes. The boys were spellbound when they sat in front of the huge screen and watched all their cartoon heroes in action. Back out on the pavement, throngs of buskers, soldiers and girls filled every street corner. Crowds of people flocked into amusement arcades with bare floorboards and rows of pinball tables. John wasted a lot of his money trying to pick up a weighed-down, silver-looking wristwatch in a glass case with a toy crane which never quite griped the watch.

John was particularly impressed by the way the American GIs could smoke and chew gum at the same time. The GIs were very generous and handed out pieces of gum to every kid in the arcade. When Ciss Bindon noticed, she made John spit out his gum.

John Bindon's first school was the strict Catholic Holy Cross in the nearby New Kings Road, where the pupils were obliged to attend Mass every day. Bindon later told friends that his memories of the school were not very good. Being a strong-willed youngster, he was regularly punished for misbehaviour, and some teachers seemed more interested in abusing the children than educating them. He was soon regularly playing truant and hanging around amusement arcades on the popular North End Road, where the daily market attracted working-class families from all over Fulham. Bindon spent much of his time playing on one-armed bandits, and was soon hooked.

Chapter One

Bindon's best friend back in those days was Barry D'Arcy. 'I had more fights than John at Holy Cross,' he later recalled. 'John had spindly thin legs and big shoulders, but he was definitely school leader in the playground. Most of us kids lived in a permanent war-footing fantasy world where you always had your raincoat done up around your neck and you raided the other schools by pretending to be Spitfires. We'd raise our arms and start swerving all over the place. Those were our wars, and I can tell you John and I won them all!'

John and his friends were the original baby boomers. 'I suppose we were the first generation to have an opinion and it showed even back when we were small kids,' says Barry. 'Miss Watson was headmistress at Holy Cross and she was considered a fair but tough character by her pupils. Mr Flanagan taught us sport and he was all right, but one teacher was a bitch and used to whack us with a ruler on the back of our legs all the time. We were also caned on the hands and back of the legs.' Both boys were given a particularly severe caning after admitting raiding the nearby Peterborough Road School where they fought pupils and then ran around the playground making a hell of a racket. John didn't have to wear a uniform after his mum told teachers the family couldn't afford to pay for one. He and others were given token shoes that were sturdy boots with thick soles and straps. 'Problem was, they marked you down as being poor, which caused a lot of aggro at school,' one of John's oldest friends later explained.

Other kids at the Holy Cross included Bindon's cousin Diane Langton who later became a well-known television actress. 'Diane had curls like Shirley Temple and she and another girl called Linda Marshall used to run after us in the playground playing kiss and chase all the time,' recalled Barry D'Arcy. And everyone noticed Ciss when she turned up at the school. 'Ciss was a very attractive lady with a lovely character, and John was clearly her pet. She'd always give him a big kiss and a hug when she came to collect him.'

Barry D'Arcy recalled one very unusual game that he played with Bindon at school. 'We'd see who could piss the highest. John's first claim to fame was that he could piss over the wall into a teacher called Mr Maloney's tea when he was on a break. He was never caught. It was hilarious.' However, when Bindon was nabbed in the loos with chewing gum, it nearly ended in agony. 'Chewing gum was an offence back in those days, so he hid it up his trousers and ended up having his nuts stuck to his leg.'

While Bindon struggled in most classroom subjects, he is still remembered to this day as an exceptional artist. He was very proud that one of his paintings of a stag's head was hung in the school hall. He also gave Barry D'Arcy his first taste of sex education, albeit slightly misguided. 'John told us babies came out when doctors cut open the sides of the women and took them out. This information soon spread round the school as we used to talk about it in the playground. Eventually we got hauled in front of the headmistress Miss Watson because kids' parents had started complaining. But Miss Watson was marvellous. She explained to us that pregnancy was one of God's gifts. It was a sacred thing and she told us all about the Virgin Mary and our Lord. But she also said we mustn't discuss it again in the playground.'

Chapter One

Pint-sized Barry D'Arcy had a lot of affinity with John Bindon because of the numerous playground scraps they both experienced. 'I used to fight all the time and I would bash up the biggest kid in the playground and that bonded me with John because he could see I stood my ground.' The 'spitfire raids' on other schools continued. 'We'd all gather outside the playgrounds and then head off in a gang of twenty. Most of us walked home from school so when we went on a raid we knew we had a bit of time on our hands because most of us were latchkey kids. We'd fly up the road in a pack. The element of surprise was essential. As we ran along the streets, our coats would be streaming in the air and we'd be gulping down Tizer, the red stuff. We must have looked quite a fearsome sight.'

The father of one of Bindon's best friends Buster Crouch owned a river pleasure boat and a lot of the boys sometimes went up the Thames to Hampton Court Palace at weekends. D'Arcy recalled, 'One time John let a woman sit down on a seat out of politeness and she turned out to own a sweet factory. John was the hero of the day because she sent out huge boxes of sweets to us all at school. That was a real lesson in manners.' On another visit to the world-famous maze at Hampton Court, Bindon and his friends feuded with a group of older school kids and slipped laxative tablets into their fizzy drinks before they went into the maze. 'That was hilarious because all these snotty kids were running around trying to find their way out in a great hurry!'

Back on the mean streets of Fulham, John's tough reputation was already growing. 'I had a problem with some kid and it seemed inevitable it would end in violence, but it didn't because John managed to calm everything down. In fact, he was very adept at avoiding violence back then,' explained Barry. 'He looked so fearsome that kids just knew to steer clear of him.' Bindon was already learning valuable lessons in life. He had become a champion of the underdog by defending the victims of school bullies. It was something that would serve him well in later life.

As soon as Bindon was old enough to cycle, he stole himself a bike and his independence immediately grew. He was naturally attracted to the river and its towpaths because of their close proximity to his home in Hugon Road, and by the time he was ten he knew virtually all the nooks and crannies near the river edge between Wandsworth and Putney Bridges. With his friends he often crossed Wandsworth Bridge to the derelict land flattened a few years earlier by the bombs, where there were huge craters the size of large swimming pools, and any remaining trees were turned into tree houses, shared with kids from nearby housing estates. There were also more secretive places away from the popular areas where old burned-out cars were turned into dens, and areas under railway arches provided another escape from grown-ups. Sometimes the Bindon brothers and their pals were chased off the bombsites by the police or other grown-ups. Bindon got his first 'pull' by the long arm of the law after being chased from a dilapidated building where he had smashed a few windows. They hauled him down to the local nick and charged him with malicious damage. He was fined by a local juvenile court and so, at just eleven years old, John Bindon already had a criminal record.

Chapter One

Back north of the river in Fulham, smaller bombsites peppered the area between the Bindon home and the busy market on the North End Road. A massive bomb had demolished a huge area on the nearby Peterborough Road, and plans to build a completely new housing estate on the site had been announced in the local *Fulham Chronicle* newspaper. A favourite haunt for John and Mickey Bindon was Scala's Ice-Cream Parlour at 387 North End Road, where they made the tastiest ice cream in west London. It was a state-of-the-art place with pale-blue, yellow and black Vitrolux tiles complete with neon lighting. Even the soda fountain and the coffee machines were chrome. Bindon would sometimes spend as long as half an hour queuing up at the kiosk for a cone. In front of Scala's was the North End Road market in all its splendour. Most of the stallholders were costermonger families who had been associated with the North End Road since the early eighteenth century. The market came alive particularly on Saturdays. Regular traders would haul their stalls to their pitches, while lorries went to Covent Garden to collect the day's fresh fruit and veg. More than 50,000 shoppers passed through the market every day, but by six o'clock in the evening the traders had packed up and gone, leaving market leftovers littering the empty street. That was when scavengers like John and Michael Bindon would appear to pick their way through the food that was lying around. Often they would manage to collect a wooden pram-load of slightly damaged fruit and veg to eat.

When Bindon's first bike was stolen, he started spending more and more time on street corners where all life passed by. Soon he was hanging around with a much older crowd of boys. London was made up of so many areas that villains were able to call their own district their 'manor'. Since the war, Fulham had earned a reputation for slippery burglars and streetwise hustlers, not to mention a family or two of very shrewd moneylenders. Characters with names like Tiger and Albert the Jar could be spotted in west London most days. Many of them also spent some of their time in Soho. Other characters worked on flower stalls and as market traders but still relished the chance to get involved in some 'business', the bigger earner the better. Fulham was ripe with opportunities for anyone with a dodgy outlook on life.

As a child, John Bindon often sat on the front doorstep of his home for hours in springtime, staring at the sky almost as if he was waiting for the clouds to disperse and the sun to come peeping through. That front step was north facing, so it was almost permanently in the shade, but occasionally a small sliver of sunlight would come shining on to his face. By 1954, people had stopped talking so much about the war and, although there were still food shortages and rationing, the streets were filled with big prams and new babies. Bindon was eleven years old, very grown up and already looking forward to leaving school and taking on the world.

His father Dennis was still in the merchant navy, and his visits home remained spasmodic, intense and filled with every range of human emotion. John Bindon's world back then was dominated by scrap metal, powdered eggs, tinned Spam and the occasional gift from some far-flung place

Chapter One

visited by his dad. When he was a young kid, it was the job of him and Michael to keep guard on the family home in Hugon Road. They were the men of the house while their father was away at sea. John would sit on that front doorstep for hours, closely scrutinising every vehicle and person who passed, including the rag-and-bone men who came trotting by on their horse and cart at least three times a day.

John was a self-contained child, happy just to sit and stare at the world going by. He wore shorts most of the time but soon grew too big for them, so in the end he made do with hand-me-down long trousers, some of which belonged to his father or uncles who lived next door in Hugon Road. His hair was cut in a pudding-bowl style, and he was tubby with a big, round face that seemed to be almost permanently smiling, especially when he was getting up to mischief. That usually occurred with the assistance of swarms of children who were drawn to the riverside area near the Bindon home. It was also when Bindon's acting career probably first kicked off. He was good at playing the tough guy even to children two or three years older than him.

Bindon's daydreams back then included a fantasy that he was in charge of a gang of criminals and they ran the area where he lived. Certainly, Bindon and his pals were in the know as far as the locality was concerned. He would often head to South Park where there were some enormous oak trees to climb. The post-war years made a strong impression on John Bindon because he had heard the tales about how there were hardly any coppers around when Hitler sent his bombers in and you could get away with all sorts of nonsense. That atmosphere still prevailed long after the war had ended. The games played by Bindon and his gang of tearaways were still based on war action featuring Brits versus the dreaded Hun. These games always started off deadly seriously but veered into farce when they got out of control. Sometimes John Bindon would overstep the mark, and a couple of his friends had to drag him off the 'enemy' on more than a few occasions.

A few yards from the Bindon home was a pub, which was the natural focal point for all the adults. Bindon's dad Dennis went there every evening when he was home from the merchant navy. Everyone in the street nodded hello, but he never engaged in much conversation. He would pull out a newspaper, lick the end of his biro with his tongue and slowly sip a pint of best while he filled in the crossword. Dennis Bindon was certainly not one of those fathers who believed that one day he would make his fortune. He might have been extremely well read, but his expectations of life were not high. He just wanted to ensure his family was provided for. Dennis was over six feet tall, well built and extremely fit, but he had no reputation as a local hard man. He wasn't interested in being a tough guy. He left that to others.

During the mid-fifties, Dennis decided he needed to acquire 'the knowledge' and start earning an income closer to home by going behind the wheel of a Hackney Carriage. It was a much more secure way to earn a living than in the merchant navy, and the tips were very good. He passed the test and his two sons were soon taking it in turns to accompany their father during long, cold days in the taxi's open luggage area, strapped in with the suitcases and coats.

But there was a darker side to Dennis Bindon. Perhaps it

Chapter One

was the result of years of frustration at not being able to cash in on his obvious intelligence. Whenever he was angry, his eyes would glaze over and Ciss would tell the children to go to their room before something bad happened. However, Ciss was more than capable of standing up to Dennis. Some of the shouting matches heard by the Bindon children shook their home to the core, but they rarely exploded into actual violence. Sometimes pieces of crockery would go flying across the kitchen and the yelling between them was filled with personal insults, but they both had strong personalities and seemed deeply in love. In those days, fighting seemed almost natural if you were born to working-class parents. It was the only way to air your grievances in front of everyone; nobody cared what the neighbours thought as they all did the same. Fisticuffs in pubs and clubs were also part of that same culture. It was usually just a punch-up followed by a handshake the next day. Fights in pubs mostly happened over a woman. Dennis Bindon never got involved as he remained the quiet drinker in the corner, but he did tend to explode in public when he felt he was being patronised by someone of a higher class than him. It was the only time he ever showed his true colours in public, and usually he would be back buried in his crossword before anyone could even offer an opinion on what he had just said.

Gradually Bindon's misdemeanours became more serious. He started thieving lead off the roofs of nearby buildings and selling it to the scrap yards, which had sprung up close to the river during the early post-war years. But beneath it all he was still a child, and he played classic street games with other children: hopscotch, skipping, Tin Tan Tommy – a glorified version of hide and seek – plus the obligatory war games, chase games and the all-time favourite: Knock Down Ginger. This required the cover of darkness, and there were only two rules: be as daring as possible and don't get caught. The rest was easy. 'You'd go down the street banging on all the doors and run away before the occupants realised it was a bunch of kids larking around,' explained Bindon's old friend Barry D'Arcy. Bindon devised a special version of the game where he would loop all the doorknockers together with string and knock an entire row at once. 'Watching all them people coming out their front doors at the same time was fucking hilarious,' Bindon said many years later.

When they weren't causing chaos out on the streets, John and Michael Bindon were both assigned specific tasks to help clean the family home. Ciss Bindon always wore an apron over her dress inside the house, together with thick, flesh-coloured stockings and beautifully polished shoes, even if she wasn't going out that day. The radio played a constant stream of the big-band tunes that were so popular just after the war. Ciss loved singing along to them at the top of her voice. That radio was one of the most important items in the Bindon household. Other friends and relatives would travel miles to spend an evening in front of the wireless. At Christmas time, dozens crowded round it listening to plays, sitcoms and royal messages wearing paper hats from the crackers pulled after a festive lunch. Throughout all this gaiety and laughter, however, Dennis Bindon would keep a low profile, occasionally joining in but usually more concerned with reading a book than playing charades.

Chapter One

It was Ciss who undoubtedly had the talent to lighten up the room. Even after three children, Ciss remained slender and attractive with well-defined cheekbones and an infectious smile. She was always immaculately dressed, even though she rarely bought any new clothes. Some members of the Bindon family said many years later that Ciss would have adored a chance to go out ballroom dancing, but Dennis Bindon was not keen on the idea so she spent most evenings in. Her and her sister's sing-songs, however, were as much a part of Bindon's life back then as cobblestones and black taxis. Sometimes one of the men would play an accordion, and there was even an upright piano that occasionally got opened up. It was here that John Bindon the performer premiered his show-business talents. He had picked up endless verses of cockney rhyming slang, together with stories and ballads passed down to him by his mother and other relatives. This was one of his favourite rhymes:

> She was walkin' down a street
> On 'er fancy plates of meat
> Wiv a summer sunshine smilin'
> Through 'er golden barnet fair.
> Bright as angels from the skies
> Wiv 'er bright-blue mutton pies
> In me east and west ol' Cupid
> Shot a shaft and left it there.

At the end of most summers, Ciss and her sisters clubbed together, hired a coach and took a few bottles of beer to the seaside: fish 'n' chips and a blustery seafront at

Southend, Margate or sometimes Brighton. The idea was to enjoy a day out on the merry-go-rounds and the big dipper and get a good whiff of sea air. But, even more importantly, these trips brought the families of Monaghan Terrace even closer together.

This was John Bindon's early life: an endless drama involving sing-songs, fights, pie and mash, bombsite playgrounds and a lot of general ducking and diving. He and his family might not have been born within the sound of Bow Bells, but they had a cockney streak nonetheless. It was a different sort of charm from today's London, but in many ways it was much more real. Back then there was still a knife-grinder on his bicycle, a chestnut-seller with his brazier of glowing coals, the Pearly King and Queen hosting a night of singing at the local, an organ-grinder with his little monkey and tin cup, old soldiers selling matches – all these characters added to the tapestry of life in the London of John Bindon's childhood. Back in those post-war years, Fulham was like a village where everyone knew everyone and neighbours still believed in helping out if you had a problem. It was a warmth that went way beyond the occasional fist fight.

Chapter Two

Bob Fifield attended the rough and ready Henry Compton secondary modern, just off the Fulham Palace Road, with Bindon. It was a vast, Victorian, red-brick building with small windows, and during the cold winter months it looked far from inviting. Fifield's first proper encounter with Bindon immediately cemented their friendship. 'I was in the toilet having a fag one day with a mate who was a stocky little fella. John came in throwing his weight around and demanded a fag. But my mate stood up to him and told him to piss off, and I thought we were in trouble. But he was very friendly then. I later learned that John was always impressed by people who stood up to him.'

If Bindon didn't want to stay in a lesson, he would just get up and leave. 'The teachers seemed a bit scared of him, so they never stopped him. I never understood why,' said

Fifield. Bindon was regularly caned, however, and Fifield never forgot the look of defiance on his face whenever he returned from being punished. 'He'd always have a broad smile on his face, almost as though he was saying they couldn't beat his spirit.'

The kids from Henry Compton were feared across Fulham as hard nuts. 'The school was the last port of call if you couldn't get into anywhere else. We were the dregs of Fulham. They used to call it "Henry's Holiday Camp" because you did so little work,' recalled Fifield. Bindon certainly made his mark at Henry Compton. One time he climbed on to the roof of the school and rang the bell. 'It was daredevil stuff, but he wasn't scared of nothing and we all treated him like a hero after that little stunt.'

Back in class, Bindon always sat at the front. 'He could be brainy when he wanted to be. He just wasn't interested in many subjects like the rest of us.' Bindon's sense of right and wrong and his protection of the victims of bullies continued. When Bob Fifield turned up to school in Wellington boots because his family were so poor, he was teased by other boys until Bindon stepped in. 'John saw them off and I never got bullied again, ever.'

By the time Bindon was thirteen, his only academic achievement was a school prize for art, and by this time he had grown out his traditional schoolboy haircut and managed a fully fledged 'Tony Curtis', which was nothing more than what was better known as a slight 'duck's arse'. Other kids were getting into the Teddy-boy scene, but as that would involve getting a suit made – probably at tailor's Mr Tobias of 200 North End Road – it was impossible for a poverty-stricken family like the Bindons.

Chapter Two

When Ciss's father Ned died, the family were obliged to sell the terrace of houses he owned. Ciss and Dennis managed to get a flat on a brand-new, much sought-after council block called Sullivan Court on the Peterborough Road, just a long stone's throw from their previous home. At first, everyone apart from Dennis hated the fourth-floor flat. It seemed more cramped and less private than their previous house; but it was their first true home together as a family. Bob Fifield was also one of the first people to move into Sullivan Court. 'It was a nice place back then. Everyone knew each other and it had a real community feeling.' There were even custom-built shops at Sullivan Court, including a laundrette, a sweet shop/newsagent, a bakery and an off-licence.

But, within weeks of moving into Sullivan Court, Bindon had one of his first 'straighteners'. 'John beat this coal man up quite badly after he had a row with him about helping deliver some bags of coal, which he did for a few bob,' recalls Fifield. When word of Bindon's victory spread around Sullivan Court, his friends gave him the nickname Biffo the Bear, after the popular *Beano* character, because 'he was round and cuddly-looking, but obviously had a hell of a punch'.

Despite living in a new tenement block, all the Bindons' old possessions still took pride of place because there was little or no money to buy replacements. The fifties might have been rocking along with a new optimism, but the Bindons were still struggling to put a meal on the table. However, that didn't stop Dennis Bindon having big plans for his children. He worked hard at furthering their knowledge even though he couldn't often afford to follow it through with actual cash. When Michael passed his common entrance exam and was offered a free scholarship to Westminster, one of London's top public schools, Dennis had to turn down the opportunity because the family couldn't even afford the school uniform and all the other expenses if Michael was to attend the school. But both John and Michael were taught from an early age that, even if you couldn't afford a special education, there were many things you could do to educate yourself.

By his early teens, John Bindon already had two female idols – Marilyn Monroe and Brigitte Bardot. He adored the way they talked in husky, whispering voices, with bodies that rolled like the surf and eyes that sparkled naughtily. Bindon wanted to be suave and sophisticated to attract such girls. The only trouble was that he didn't really know how to handle them. He had been kissing and cuddling and fooling around at the back of a few bike sheds, but now he was thinking about what it would be like to go the whole way. He adopted a macho walk like his tough-guy screen idol Robert Mitchum. This meant keeping his shoulders back and head held high, and it had the effect of making him seem much older than he really was. But there was one part of his anatomy that Bindon was growing extremely proud of, and which undoubtedly contributed to his obsession with dating girls. He summed it up many years later when he told one interviewer, 'My mum used to give me a right-hander for showing it off as a kid. It was big even then!'

Bindon's twelve-inch penis had already provoked much comment whenever he was in the showers after school sports days, and, even though he was only just fourteen, he

Chapter Two

was already spending time at local pubs drinking beer where his favourite party trick would emerge, a routine used many times in pubs across the world over the following forty years. 'I'd hang five half-pint beer glasses on me manhood. Everyone would ask how it's done beforehand so I'd put them out of their misery and thread my old chap through the handles of the glasses.' He would also sometimes dip his penis in people's glasses while saying, 'He needs a drink!'

Not surprisingly, Bindon's strong appearance and brash nature soon led to numerous scraps in and around Fulham, but he never lost his outrageous sense of humour. On one occasion he was having breakfast at home in Sullivan Court when he dropped something on to a plate of bacon and eggs his brother Michael was eating. Afterwards, Bindon claimed it was another man's ear he had bitten off during a fight the previous evening. No one argued with him about the claim, and Michael was understandably upset about what he'd eaten. As one old friend said many years later, 'That was Big John's favourite gag, and the thing is that no one ever dared challenge him on it, in case it was true.'

But beneath Bindon's jokey exterior still lay a highly sensitive lad. He was particularly upset about any comments relating to the size of his head, which was quite big in comparison to the rest of his body. As a youngster, he was known to have sometimes banged his own head against a wall or a door in frustration. 'Some people reckoned John was deformed because of the size of his head and his huge dick,' one old friend explained, 'and he used to get very upset if he heard anyone talking about him that way.'

Some kids gave Bindon a wide berth, saying, 'Poor old Biff, he's a bit wonky.' Bindon soon lashed out at the taunters and began calling himself Big Louis after a character in one of his favourite films, the original *Scarface*.

Other examples of Bindon's softer side suggest a young man in emotional turmoil. His cousin Gordon Wilson explained, 'Sometimes he got upset purely because he'd hurt someone's feelings in the family. Once he played a practical joke on one of my brothers by pushing an ice cream into his face when he was eating. Usually we'd all laugh about it, but my brother wasn't in a very good mood and he pushed it away and had a right go at Johnny. They both got quite angry and we all expected Johnny to say, "Shut up or shape up," or something like that, but he didn't say a word. Then he just looked at my mum and burst out crying. There he was, the toughest bloke I've ever known in my life, built like a brick shithouse, and he's sobbing. Then he walked out of the house and my mum said someone should go and get him before he did some serious damage to anyone who happened to walk past him. He was like a tinderbox. If anyone said anything to him it would set him off.' Eventually Gordon's brothers found Bindon and brought him back to their house. 'Soon they were all back laughing and joking again. Afterwards, I realised John had dropped his guard for a split second and that was why he'd cried.' Gordon never forgot how friends of his older brothers were in awe of Bindon even back then. 'They were scared of him. They knew his reputation and often you'd hear people saying they'd gone to get a drink and spotted Bindon in there and that had worried them. At that age I didn't appreciate just how hard he really was.'

Chapter Two

Every Christmas day, the Wilsons hosted a party at their house in Fernhurst Road, Fulham. Ciss always came, but usually without Dennis. 'Parties just weren't Dennis's cup of tea,' said Gordon. Indeed, Dennis was an enigma to the Wilson family. 'He was very reserved and very shy, but he could sit you down and explain everything to you in a patient manner. He seemed to know about every subject that you talked about. He could explain why you did this and why you did that. It was always very personal and he made you feel important when he told you.'

Back at Sullivan Court, Dennis had his own den, into which no one was allowed to venture. 'It was his escape hatch, I suppose,' says Gordon. 'He kept all his newspapers and books and stuff in there, and would often retreat into that room for hours on end. It was his sanctuary. I remember as a kid we weren't allowed in there. But I can tell you Dennis was one of the most honourable men I've ever met in my life, and he never showed off. He's such a private man in many ways and I suppose Johnny's antics over the years made him feel a little uncomfortable.'

Dennis was disappointed when John left school at fourteen without any real qualifications. He had genuinely hoped that either John or Michael would make it to university. But Bindon had learned at least one valuable lesson at school. He had become a champion of the underdog by regularly defending the victims of school bullies, and he told friends he would never stand by and watch people 'having the piss taken out of them'. He told one pal, 'I've got a useful pair of fists and I intend to use them if necessary. There's a lot of people out there who need characters like me.'

Bindon spent the first few months after leaving school roaming the streets and dance halls. There were three main venues that he regularly visited: the Hammersmith Palais, the Wimbledon Palais and Fulham Town Hall. His social life went from strength to strength as he took girlfriends to the cinema, restaurants and coffee bars. Making love had become a regular occurrence and sometimes John would sneak a girl into the family flat on the Peterborough Estate while his dad was out in his cab and Ciss was out cleaning. On other occasions, Bindon would persuade his latest conquest to accompany him to South Park where they would have 'a kiss and a cuddle' behind one of the vast oak trees that backed on to the two main football pitches.

As John's confidence grew, and the 1950s became the 1960s, he began taking expeditions further up the King's Road, which exposed him to a new crowd of laid-back people, many of whom were in the fast-expanding media world. He even persuaded one TV producer he met to let him appear in the backing crowd for Adam Faith's performance on *6.5 Special*, a weekly dose of pop music that went out live on television at five past six every Saturday evening from the Shepherds Bush Theatre. Bindon was fascinated by celebrity guests including Billy Fury, Eden Kane, Jess Conrad, P. J. Proby and Marty Wilde with their slicked-back hairstyles, snaking hips and tight trousers. He particularly liked the rockers. They had a sort of hard-man, seen-it-all world-weariness to them, and slid about on stage before driving off home in their big American gas-guzzlers. Long hair, flower power and LSD weren't yet on the scene.

Bindon later said that what particularly intrigued him

Chapter Two

about the stars on *6.5 Special* was that they enjoyed a jar or two and seemed very happy just cruising along on a wave of rock 'n' roll. He related to most of them because they were all working-class kids making a name for themselves. They were part of an entire generation spearheading the opening of doors into music, films, literature, screenwriting, photography and all the artistic pursuits that had once been the private domain of the wealthy. In addition, the big boys like Adam Faith, Marty Wilde and Billy Fury seemed to have the pick of the women – and that was something John Bindon definitely wanted a piece of. The groupie scene was just emerging and, when Bindon heard stories about girls throwing themselves at these rock 'n' rollers, it filled him with envy. An endless supply of birds and booze – it sounded like heaven to a lively teenager, already proud of the size of his manhood.

But all this was cruelly interrupted when John was caught stealing crates of beer from the local British Legion club in Parsons Green, and ended up in the long arms of the local law once again. Bindon always later claimed it was nothing more than a harmless prank, but at Fulham nick they decided to throw the book at him and he ended up in a local magistrates' court where he got three months in borstal for theft. Bindon later tried to make light of his incarceration, and even told his mates he enjoyed making mailbags while in custody. He learned how to sew, and even used a special type of stitch which he proudly announced was 'the old mailbag stitch'. Ironically, it was while he was in borstal that Bindon discovered something he had never experienced in the outside world. A few of the other inmates were smoking cannabis, and when he tried a puff he found it rather pleasant. He especially liked the way that pot helped calm him down when he was feeling tense.

Bindon's early criminal record is steeped in rumour and gossip, but it is clear that shortly after his release from borstal he got nicked again with a Fulham pal called Alan Stanton. This time it was for taking and driving away a car, and possessing live ammunition. He was given a one-year term inside, and while serving his time he met a bunch of other young criminals who believed the only way to make big bucks was to join the underworld full-time. Bindon and Stanton – a pint-sized character with a short temper and an intense stare – were regularly called up in front of the governor for disciplinary offences. Stanton said many years later that he was often victimised by the wardens because of his size and that Bindon regularly came to his rescue. One of Stanton's oldest friends later explained, 'Alan never forgot the way John helped him while they were in borstal together, and they stayed friends as a result.'

In the middle of their sentences, Bindon and Stanton were transferred by prison bus to another borstal. En route, Stanton managed to slip out of his handcuffs because he had such small wrists. He then disappeared through the window of the prison van into the middle of London. Minutes later, he stole a car and drove past the prison bus where Bindon was still sitting at the same window. Stanton's friend explained, 'When the screws asked where the little one had gone, John told them he had just waved at him from a passing car.' He was caught two weeks later and his sentence doubled. Stanton – a habitual

Chapter Two

'bolter' – was the only person Bindon ever allowed to call him 'Big Head', because they both later tried to break out of a borstal cell but changed their minds when Bindon couldn't get his head through the window.

Back in Fulham after his release, Bindon's fast-growing reputation as a hard man led to him working as an enforcer (debt collector) for a number of heavyweight criminals, even though he was still relatively young. There were also rumours that some local teams of blaggers used him to smash down glass screens in banks because of his extraordinary strength, although Bindon himself never hung around for the actual robberies. 'He always said he never had the bottle for the blaggings,' Alan Stanton later told a friend.

Less than two years later, Bindon was sentenced to another term in prison, this time for living off the immoral earnings of a prostitute, although he always claimed he did the one-year sentence for a friend and even got handsomely paid in the process. 'John was no pimp. He just did a favour for a friend and got well paid in the process,' explained one old pal. Intriguingly, many years later Bindon insisted he had been in love with the woman who was working as a prostitute. 'I was infatuated with her. She was a much older woman and very attractive. I was intrigued by what she did.'

No sooner was Bindon out of borstal on that charge than he got twenty-one months for attacking three Scotsmen with a broken bottle and was sent to Maidstone Prison. A definite pattern was emerging in John Bindon's life: he was fast becoming what the police called a career criminal.

Shortly after getting out of prison, Bindon got together with an attractive married woman called Sheila Davies.

Sheila already had children and a husband – a renowned armed robber – but none of that stopped the teenage Bindon. Whenever there was a problem with any of Sheila's husband's friends, Bindon let it be known he had 'once cut a geezer's hand off' and then delivered the hand in a box to his victim the next day. It earned him a measure of respect.

The one thing Bindon had discovered earlier in borstal which wasn't related to crime was rugby. He started playing for a number of clubs, including the London Springboks, the Public Schools and the Law Society. Bindon was a perfectly built prop forward, complete with square shoulders, shortish legs and a propensity for violence that found the perfect outlet on the rugby fields of London. On one occasion, he also turned out for his cousin Alan's Sunday football team when they played a team from the Metropolitan Police. Cousin Gordon Wilson remembered, 'These coppers were known for giving a lot of stick to everyone. John was rubbish at football, but Alan got him to play purely for one reason. They had this really big ginger copper starring for them. He must have been at least six foot five and used to terrorise everyone. No one was big enough to tackle this giant. But the moment the whistle went, Johnny just ran the length of the field until he got to this bloke, then he smashed into him, knocking him over and said under his breath, "Now you know what I'm here for." There were no more problems with that copper after that, and we won the game!'

One of Bindon's favourite watering holes was The Britannia pub, on the corner of Britannia Road and Fulham Road, just opposite Chelsea Football Club's Stamford Bridge stadium. Later, he even moved his lover

Chapter Two

Sheila Davies into a flat just opposite the pub. The Britannia was the sort of local pub that villains flocked to. As Fred Hayes – son of the then landlords George and Nora Hayes – later recalled, 'One night Bindon had a row with a guy called Scotch Andy, and my old man told him to have a fight round the back of the pub instead of inside so the filth weren't called.' Bindon settled the fight with a flurry of right-handers and then went back to Sheila, who was more than capable of looking after herself. 'Sheila could handle Bindon. She wasn't afraid of him and they had a good thing going,' recalled Fred.

Bindon said many years later that from the moment he met Sheila Davies he was only happy when they were together, and many believe she was the main love of his life. He even told one drinking pal in The Britannia that he dreamed of spending the rest of his life with her. But none of Bindon's friends at the time expected it to last.

Occasional jobs as an enforcer only provided Bindon with beer money, so when a close pal called Johnny Gillette suggested he join him doing smudge work – photographing tourists outside Buckingham Palace – he jumped at the chance. But he found it difficult to keep his temper with many of the tourists, so he decided to try some 'normal' work instead. He laid asphalt, plucked pheasants and then got himself a job with an antique dealer on the King's Road.

At work, Bindon spent the whole time counting down the hours to when he could see Sheila again. Back at the family home in Sullivan Court, he would retreat to the only bathroom and fight off angry knocks while he prepared himself for Sheila. One time he ironed a pair of trousers five times just to make sure there were no creases. The pair often spent their nights out boozing in The Britannia before retiring to the flat together opposite for bouts of steamy sex. Bindon showered Sheila with tiny gifts: a simple rose in a plastic box, French chocolates or even perfume. Some nights they would sit together in the corner of The Britannia sipping slowly on their drinks and snogging like a pair of lovesick puppies.

It was Sheila Davies who first introduced Bindon to cooking. With Ciss at home, he had never been allowed anywhere near the kitchen, but Sheila was more than happy to encourage her young lover to develop his culinary skills. Bindon eventually persuaded Ciss to divulge some of her Irish recipes, but his favourite dish of all was cassoulet with sausages and bacon. 'He'd cook it to absolute perfection, taking hours to get it all right,' explained one former girlfriend many years later.

By now John Bindon had a reputation for violence. Money was still so tight that he didn't own a suit, so his brother Michael would lend him his on condition he didn't get any blood on it ...

Chapter Three

Bindon's reputation as a hard man was soon spreading way beyond Fulham. 'People would turn up in some local pubs from all over London to challenge Johnny,' explained cousin Gordon Wilson. 'Some were from as far afield as Deptford or the East End, and they all reckoned they could have him. Johnny was a scary-looking fella back then, and spoke with a deep gruff voice and growled a lot. He never bragged about being a tasty fighter, but you only had to look at him to see it was true.'

But, then, Fulham had a reputation, as south-London criminal legend Freddie Foreman explained years later. 'I used to go down there with a crew from Bermondsey. We'd visit this late-night coffee stall and one of my pals Patsy would offer to fight any man. These Fulham lads would step out bold as brass. I'd hold their coats while Patsy got a pasting. Next thing I know, they're kicking me all over the road. It was like, "On yer knees, have you had enough?" Then we'd get up, shake hands and go and get a sausage sandwich. That was what it was like back then.'

There were some truly tough characters coming through the ranks in Fulham – Brian Emmett, Lennie and Ronnie Osborne, Eddie Cox and a family of brothers called the Edwards to name but a few. Bindon was still scraping a living doing debt-collecting work for local villains and winning a few bob in unofficial pub prize fights, so it wasn't surprising when, in 1964, Bindon got arrested yet again – this time for assault, actual bodily harm and wounding after he got involved in a bust-up in a pub. He was sentenced to two years.

But by now, jail held little fear for a hardened character like John Bindon. In later years, he adored retelling stories of his survival in prison. One classic tale comes courtesy of the great man himself: 'I was in a cell at Wandsworth, and you're not allowed to have anything in the cell and you have a see-through potty to piss in. It was fuckin' miserable so I decided to have some fun. At breakfast I nicked two sausages and some lemon juice and went back to my cell. Later that day they was coming around to slop out and the screws would creep along the corridors in case you were wanking and then they'd shout, "Spin it!", then spin the key and open up the door and hope to catch you at it. I was well fed up of this sort of outrageous behaviour so when the screw came into my cell I picked up the potty and started drinking the lemon juice and then picked up one of the brown bangers which they thought was my own shit and started eating it. They soon left me alone after that.'

But there were more serious incidents inside. One of

Chapter Three

Bindon's pals was in the showers at Wandsworth and someone had put razor blades in the soap. 'Poor bastard cut himself to pieces. That was really out of order,' said Bindon many years later.

At Wandsworth, Bindon encountered a notorious inmate called Frank 'Mad Axeman' Mitchell, one of the hardest criminals of his era. He had been one of the Kray twins' most trusted 'soldiers' until his imprisonment. Bindon looked up to Frank Mitchell, whom he considered to be a big star; Mitchell, in turn, was flattered by Bindon's attention and eventually introduced him to the Krays when they visited him in prison. Mitchell had virtual hero status inside Wandsworth. He was a genuine face who had even been punished with the cat-o'-nine-tails after regularly clashing with screws. Prison staff were terrified of him, and the screws tried to avoid going into his cell alone. Mitchell seemed to rule whatever jail he happened to be in. In the prison gym, he was as strong as an ox and thrived on always doing more exercises than anyone else – he would even have two people on his back while he did press-ups. Mitchell could also pick up a piano and arm-wrestle everyone to the ground in seconds. The Kray twins made sure Mitchell got money, and even laid on women for him when he was outside the prison on a working party. When he was at one prison outside London, he was even spotted in the local pub after treating everyone to a drink. To cap it all, the so-called 'Mad Axeman' had a couple of budgies in his cell!

Bindon quickly became one of Mitchell's most trusted runners, and happily fetched and carried for him. To some it must have seemed bizarre that young John Bindon would be so impressed by a thirty-seven-year-old whose intractability and violence over twenty years of barely interrupted imprisonment had seen him escape five times and earned him that 'Mad Axeman' nickname from the tabloids. If Mitchell wasn't picking fights himself, his awesome reputation meant that some prison officer or other always wanted to put him in his place. One prison report on Mitchell stated, 'We have gone as far as we can go with him. Mitchell is now like a man steadily walking towards the horizon and yet finding he is getting no nearer to it. The suspicion is beginning to dawn on him that he never will reach it.'

Mitchell's request for a release date kept being turned down by the Home Office. At first he had been optimistic, but, as year followed year without any date materialising, his mood changed to resignation. Bindon shared in his frustration at the rejection letters that offered no tangible explanation. By late 1965, Mitchell's only visitors were the Kray twins, and they too shared in his frustration and even pledged to get him home whatever it took. Bindon left Wandsworth around that time and, a year later, Mitchell escaped from Dartmoor Prison with the help of the Krays. However, they then turned on him, labelled him a liability and had him killed while he was on the run.

As Bindon walked out of Wandsworth on his release, one of the screws said to him, 'I won't say goodbye because you'll be back.'

Bindon's response was typically strong-willed: 'I was fuckin' determined to prove him wrong.'

Tough guy John Bindon, hardest man in west London, had come to a crossroads in his life. He had spent more

Chapter Three

than half the previous six years in jail and he didn't like it. The clever ones were the people who stayed out of nick. Crime was a short-term solution. He needed a career away from all those familiar, risky temptations. The first thing he did on his release was try and find himself a new home away from all of Fulham's shady characters. He tapped up Paddy Kennedy, the legendary Irish landlord of The Star in Belgravia, about a tiny mews house that belonged to the pub and had lain empty for years. Kennedy had always had a soft spot for Bindon, and agreed to rent it to him for a peppercorn £2 a week. Bindon immediately gave it a swift paint job inside and out, and got his brother Michael and others to help replumb the toilet and kitchen. However, he decided not to put in a proper bathroom because, as Bindon said many years later, 'I wanted to make sure none of the young ladies in my life got the idea they might want to move in with me.'

Now settled with a home in an upmarket location, he set about the job of conquering the other side of west London. Things had certainly changed since his first spell inside prison.

A century of prudery had been overturned by the *Lady Chatterley* trial. Satire boomed and the Profumo scandal was just the tip of the moral iceberg. Then England triumphed in the World Cup at Wembley in 1966, and anti-war protestors stormed the US Embassy in Grosvenor Square. Along came Twiggy, Mary Quant, David Hockney, Sandie Shaw and Harold Wilson. In the freezing winter of 1962–3 in a back room in a rundown hotel in Richmond in the London suburbs, the Rolling Stones started their rise to fame. British cinema was booming in a more daring artistic direction than Hollywood. In the London theatre, Pinter and Osborne had supplanted Coward and Rattigan. On television, *That Was The Week That Was* provided opportunities for comedians to lampoon entrenched attitudes. Comic genius Peter Cook, one of the infamous *Beyond The Fringe* quartet, co-founded the satirical fortnightly *Private Eye* and even opened a Soho nightclub called The Establishment.

But much of the evolution of the swinging Sixties was down to fashion – and the King's Road was where it was at. Just down the road from John Bindon's family home was a netherworld of rising hemlines; girls abandoned stockings and girdles for pantyhose. John Bindon's manor had not only become a centre for boutiques with names such as Skin, Granny Takes a Trip and Stop the Shop, but was also a veritable fashion catwalk for all-comers. Back then, fashion photographers were the latest heroes, but their work went far beyond the glamour magazines. Celebrities of the day – from movie stars to the Kray twins, whose reign of terror hadn't yet ended in life sentences – posed readily for them. Glamour had edged its way into crime and vice versa. Photographers like David Bailey were at the centre of this twisted universe. Italian film director Michelangelo Antonioni located Chelsea to make *Blow Up*, its central figure a photographer played by David Hemmings.

Into this potent mix came illegal substances including LSD, which allegedly opened the eyes of many. At middle-class dinner parties cannabis joints started to be passed round regularly. When Mick Jagger was arrested and

Chapter Three

given a suspended jail sentence for drugs, it was clear that what was left of the Establishment was trying to make an example of him. In the King's Road, everyone who was anyone hung out at places like the Picasso café, the Chelsea Potter and Alvaro's restaurant. Boutique owner (and later bestselling novelist) Pat Booth – who knew Bindon well – opened up a whole block of trendy shops. 'There were still a few dodgy characters around but that was part of the appeal of the place,' says Pat Booth today. 'Everyone knew everybody else and that's why we crossed all the class divides so smoothly. Men came to the King's Road to check out all the pretty girls without getting into trouble. I always employed the best-looking girls to lure them all into my shops.'

Suddenly it didn't matter what background you came from. The so-called 'posh birds' went out of their way to find a bit of rough and vice versa. As Pat Booth explained, 'People like Bindon never found me attractive because we came from the same type of working-class background. We were both looking for something above our station. Look, we were all having fun back then, real fun. It wasn't about drugs because they hadn't taken a grip yet. I certainly didn't do any and the criminals like John Bindon were more interested in girls and boozing.'

More importantly, girls were now on the pill for the first time, which meant they were prepared to have affairs with men without needing to get married. Pat Booth recalls, 'There was an awful lot of sexual promiscuity going on, but at least the class barriers had come down. A rich girl could go out with a working-class man without any repercussions.' For the first time ever, women were earning more than their parents were and in some cases supporting their families. 'It was a total climate change and the Bindons and all those guys took complete advantage of the situation. Who can blame them?'

On a typical Saturday afternoon, the King's Road was a magnet for the so-called beautiful people. 'It was the promenade of Europe,' says Pat Booth. 'These young people came to be seen at the right places.' An assortment of men would drive along the King's Road in their MGBs and E-Types. Among the famous young stars on parade back then were Terence Stamp, David Hemmings and Michael Caine. Sometimes John Lennon would float by with his first wife Cynthia, and Paul McCartney often mulled around in one of Pat Booth's boutiques.

One of the first posh clubs that Bindon went to was a jazz club called Cy Laurie's on the King's Road where almost everyone was smoking pot and gulping down purple hearts so they could stay awake all night. Back where he came from, it was fine to pickle yourself on barrels of booze, but class-A drugs were considered the devil's candy and he steered well clear of them. Cannabis was fine to help calm him down, he thought, but he wasn't going touch any of that 'heavy shit' like cocaine and heroin. Back in his family home at Sullivan Court, Bindon was still the working-class son trying to mend his ways for the sake of his parents who were worried about his criminal connections. They had no idea he had experimented with the dreaded weed. Their only knowledge of drugs was the shock-horror headlines in the tabloids which implied that cannabis was poisonous stuff which made people go crazy.

Chapter Three

John Bindon had been slipping in and out of two totally diverse worlds: there was his old familiar manor of Fulham, where ducking and diving remained relatively easy, while less than a mile up the King's Road lay an exotic, tempting, attractive universe. Bindon wasn't sure if he actually wanted to take the final leap, and for the moment remained with one foot firmly planted in both worlds.

There were also some heavy characters from other parts of London who wanted words with John Bindon. One face who had been upset by him was south-London criminal Joey Pyle, who marched into Bindon's favourite boozer, The Britannia, on a mission to destroy him. 'I'd heard he'd been saying things about me which I didn't like the sound of. So I sent a message to Bindon to come and see me, but he never turned up, which was disappointing. So I headed for The Britannia.'

Pyle went straight up to Bindon in the middle of the pub frequented by all John's pals and said, 'I heard you been saying things about me. What you gonna fuckin' do about it?'

Bindon immediately denied bad-mouthing Pyle, but later admitted he'd been expecting a thrashing despite his plea of innocence. Pyle accepted Bindon's word and the two men formed an unlikely alliance. 'From that day on we became good pals,' Pyle later recalled. 'I got to like John Bindon a lot. He was running around getting into trouble and certainly making a name for himself. I knew that John could handle himself, and he knew the same about me. From my point of view he was a lovely bloke. I never saw no wrong in him. The Kray twins also had a lot of respect for him.'

Pyle told how the Krays paid Bindon to 'sort out a problem' they had with a Fulham man who hadn't paid them back a large debt. 'That was the kind of relationship he had with the Twins,' says Pyle. 'John did what he had to do. It was left to John to decide how to resolve the problem. It wouldn't be a kiss on the cheek, I can tell you that.' Pyle was soon very impressed. 'Bindon done a few jobs for me. He was good like that. He wasn't greedy. He liked a few bob, but he'd never take the piss. He handled himself very well and was very fit and strong.'

Meanwhile, in Bindon's 'other life' in the trendy surroundings of the Sloane Square end of the King's Road, he came across the only hard man who would eventually compete with him in terms of his lifestyle and penchant for bedding rich and famous women. George Wright was a streetwise cockney who had gatecrashed high society, and who had had a stormy relationship with a titled lady. As one of George Wright's posh lovers later explained, 'George was different. He wasn't a deb's delight, a chinless wonder. He was physically very strong and masculine. And he was totally unpredictable.'

Wright was a rough diamond with a penchant for smart suits and clever patter, which had seen him become king of Warren Street, London's second-hand-car Mecca. But he and Bindon crossed swords on a number of occasions, and Wright deeply disapproved of the way Bindon was trying to muscle in on his territory. They ended up having a face-off at The Star pub in Belgravia when Bindon tried to pick up a girl who was with Wright. Insults were exchanged and knives flashed, but it fizzled out without either side resorting to violence. Joe Pyle insists that Bindon regularly

Chapter Three

tried to avoid aggravation. 'John was a good enforcer and a good guy to have on your side. He wasn't a workaholic and he wanted to avoid the nick, while it was part of life for most heavyweight criminals.'

One member of the upmarket King's Road set whom Bindon encountered at this time was budding socialite Anthony Rufus-Isaacs. He recalled, 'Bindon was this good-looking guy, and back in the sixties there were loads of hoods and lots of posh girls who wanted to bed a bit of rough.'

Many of Rufus-Isaacs's titled lady friends deliberately engineered meetings with tough guys like Bindon and George Wright expressly to go to bed with them. 'It was all a bit of a game to these women when they began moving in on the ruffians, so to speak. Wright and Bindon often competed for the same girls, and it did lead to a few problems between them.'

Wright had even managed to acquire the lease to a house on a lord's country estate; of course, Bindon had his own version of that with the rented mews house in Belgravia. 'I remember Bindon turning up for dinner parties,' recalled Rufus-Isaacs, 'and stirring the moose with his prick. We all thought he was hilarious, if a little scary at times. Other times he'd be in a pub and would get a girl to give him a hard-on and then thread the beer mugs on the end of his prick for his famed party trick.'

Rufus-Isaacs was friendly with the blonde sister of George Wright's girlfriend Sally Hodge. She was called Vicki Hodge, but he nicknamed her Tricky Vicki. 'I'd actually known her since she came out as a debutante. Tricky Vicki was very pretty and very saucy with short skirts and wonderful long legs, but even then I knew she was very manipulative. She didn't give anything away for nothing.' Vicki Hodge clearly had her eyes on Bindon and was annoyed with Rufus-Isaacs for not bothering to introduce them at a dinner party they all attended.

'It was just a mad, mad time full of incredible excesses,' Rufus-Isaacs sums it up. 'Everyone was drunk and shagging every night and everyone was on supercharge. I don't know how we all did it but there was a lot of money around. George Wright seemed to have wads of cash and used to bring out Cartier watches and lighters, whatever you wanted. I still have my Cartier – I paid him £100 for it.' And Bindon had in a sense become Rufus-Isaacs's court jester. 'He was such a laugh and would always be game for just about anything. He'd get his dick out and stick it in Lady whatever's hair, then we'd all fall about laughing. That's how he earned his supper.'

Bindon's new upmarket crowd of King's Road cronies encouraged him to continue playing rugby, and he became a highly rated prop forward for the London Springboks. One of his best friends in the team was a gigantic South African lock called Ronnie Tomlinson, who looked like the singer Glen Campbell. One night he and Bindon had a drunken fight outside The Star that lasted half an hour. Bindon later insisted that afterwards they both declared a draw and bonded as friends for life.

Another close pal he made at this time was a young American actor called Bennie Carruthers who claimed descent from the first Mexican president, but had decided to make his living in London from the mid-1960s. His first role on British TV came in the Troy Kennedy Martin thriller *On The Run*. Carruthers always claimed his

Chapter Three

education came on New York's mean streets and that a lucky break landed him in the lead on a Broadway show. He was the first real actor John Bindon had ever encountered, and he enthused non-stop about the job, even suggesting that Bindon – with his real 'tough' background – would make a great thespian. Bindon laughed at first because back where he came from actors were considered 'fuckin' poofs', and the idea of being one had genuinely never crossed his mind.

Another working-class character called Billy Murray had mentioned his acting aspirations to his mentors the Krays, and they had financed his enrolment into drama school. Murray had grown up on the mean streets of Forest Gate, east London, and left school at fifteen before the Twins took him under their wing because of their mutual love of boxing. Murray even helped them out by doing the odd stint of painting and decorating for them. He came across Bindon in a wine bar called The Nose in Sloane Square and also encouraged him to think seriously about treading the boards. 'Bindon had this aura about him,' Murray recalled, 'even back then, and I thought that if he could transfer that character into acting he could be a phenomenal performer. Bindon used to hold court at The Nose, and I would see him down a club called The Bag o' Nails in Kingly Street in the West End. I liked him – he was loud and cracked a lot of jokes. Bindon had a reputation even back then as a tough guy, but he was never affiliated to any particular crowd. We became mates and used to meet and go out. He'd walk past the bouncers at any door and they'd let him in with no rows.'

One night, Bindon and Murray went down to a

notorious West Indian club in the West End. 'We were well pissed and the only white people in there. Bindon knew it was a heavy place so, as a show of strength, he high-kicked the ceiling from standstill as we walked in. The locals were stunned and gave us no aggro whatsoever that evening. Bindon loved showing off. He had the biggest, broadest smile you've ever seen in your life – a big set of white teeth. He was a performer even back then.'

But for the moment, Bindon needed to earn some decent money. So when his old Fulham pal Alan Stanton mentioned there might be a bit of dodgy work on the horizon, Bindon couldn't resist it. He agreed to join a three-man team who had planned the robbery of a Hatton Garden gems dealer. Stanton couldn't do the job himself because he was too short to be sufficiently threatening to pull off the blag.

The story begins in the modest Hatton Garden office, where emerald expert Raymond Taghioff works to this day. 'I was contacted by a man who wanted to buy a specific emerald,' he explained, 'so I went to the Grosvenor Hotel to deliver the stone after I'd checked the buyer out through an intermediary. The man was supposed to be at the hotel with £20,000 to pay for it, but when I knocked on the door of his hotel suite I was held up by three men with guns. The other man was nowhere to be seen and I was immediately relieved of my stone at gunpoint. I did chase after them when they ran off, but I lost them in the crowds outside.'

Seasoned south-London villain Mickey Blackmore was arrested after being stopped by police on a routine traffic violation the following day. Officers found a bullet behind

Chapter Three

the back seat and then discovered Mr Taghioff's bag in the boot. Bindon was later detained by police, but Taghioff failed to identify him in a line-up, so he was released. In addition, the police did not have enough evidence to charge the man who set up the crime in the first place. He was a wealthy fence with close contacts to Alan Stanton, which was how Bindon got involved. Another of the robbers was eventually arrested, but got off after he produced witnesses who claimed he was somewhere else at the time. Mr Taghioff still vividly remembers the emerald. 'It was an old mining stone and a very fine nineteen carat. It took me thirteen years to pay off that stone after it was stolen, so it caused me a lot of problems. You could say it changed my life.' Today that emerald would be worth at least £1 million.

Many believe that all those involved in the crime came under the curse of the emerald: Blackmore was later killed by a hit man; Stanton died in tragic circumstances; the so-called fixer of the crime was eventually jailed for another murder; and as for Bindon – well, we shall see ...

Peter McGoohan was a young detective constable investigating the emerald robbery. He remains convinced to this day that the stone is cursed. 'Over in Fulham I even told the local detectives that if they ever found the emerald they should keep their hands off it because otherwise they'd end up cursed. I never believed in such stuff before then, but the fact remains that so many of these characters' lives ended dramatically.'

McGoohan interviewed Bindon at Gerald Road Police Station. 'I remember him well. He was young, same age as me – mid-twenties. And never stopped smiling from the minute he came in the nick. He just kept saying, "You're havin a laugh, ain't ya?" We had to let him go in the end.'

Afterwards, Bindon went out to The Britannia for a celebration drink and swore he would never get sucked into any more robberies as long as he lived. 'John just didn't have the right mentality to pull off such jobs. It didn't give him the sort of buzz professional robbers feel. Alan Stanton told him to walk away and never get involved in such crimes ever again,' explained one of Stanton's oldest friends many years later.

Just a few weeks after getting away with that robbery, Bindon got a call from one of his new King's Road media friends, a writer called Nell Dunn. Years later Bindon recalled, 'She asked me out for a drink to meet a film director called Ken Loach and a casting director. She wanted to recommend me for the job as technical adviser for a film called *Poor Cow*. I knew all the south-London slum location spots where they were going to film like I knew the inside of Wandsworth. The next day, Nell told me I'd got a part in the film as well as the job as technical adviser. I said, "What kind of part?" Because apart from the fact I'd just got a good job as an antique totter [door-to-door buyer], if it was just a bit-part my chums would take the mickey, and then I'd be back in the punch-up business.'

Nell assured Bindon it was one of the starring roles, and so Bindon began work on *Poor Cow* in the middle of 1967. His co-star was one of the few actors he already knew: Krays prodigy Billy Murray. Murray couldn't help but be impressed by the rookie actor. 'I remember Bindon saying he'd met someone called Ken Loach who wanted him to be

Chapter Three

in a movie. There was I straight out of acting school, and he'd copped a huge role without ever acting a sentence. But even then John didn't seem to have any nerves. He wasn't scared of a camera or anyone, directors or producers. He treated everyone exactly the same and he loved the fact that being an actor would open doors to attractive women and glamorous parties. He was in his element. I suppose in a way he'd been acting for years before Ken Loach came alone. Loach adored him. Meanwhile, I ended up with hardly anything in the film after Terence Stamp came in and took the main part I'd originally been promised. I ended up just one of the gang in one scene. But that's show business, I guess.'

The female lead in *Poor Cow* was an established young actress called Carol White, who came from a very similar background to Bindon. Her father Joe had been a market spieler, a rag-and-bone man and a prize fighter. He was a big, powerful man who was feared on his manor. Carol White's name was already synonymous with swinging London – long hair, mini-skirts and the Beatles. *Cathy Come Home* had turned her into a household name. But, while Carol and Bindon may have shared similar backgrounds, they were poles apart when it came to the acting game. She already considered herself a celebrity who had dined with the likes of Brigitte Bardot, Rudolf Nureyev, Clint Eastwood and Dudley Moore. Bindon was a first-timer, a rough diamond who probably reminded Carol White just a little too much of herself. Carol's other co-star on *Poor Cow*, Terence Stamp, was a former lover, which meant that any other actor on set was sure to feel a little left out, although Bindon later insisted he never noticed a problem.

Bindon's role in *Poor Cow* stirred up a lot of press interest, if only because he was a jailbird in a profession still dominated by public schoolboys from safe, secure, middle- and upper-class backgrounds. The London *Evening Standard* even claimed Bindon only got the part because his easy-going exterior hid a hardcore penchant for violence and an utter disregard for the law. As the newspaper commented, 'Mr Bindon seems to fit the part very well. A seemingly gentle man with a good deal of high charm, he has spent seven of his twenty-four years in jail, mostly for acts of violence. He is also not very fond of policemen.'

Bindon himself admitted to one reporter, 'The husband's environment and attitudes in *Poor Cow* are just like mine. The only thing which is out of character is that I have to hit Carol White in one scene – and I never hit women. And everything I say in the play, I mean – including the bits about the police. I had no script and was allowed to say anything I liked, except profanities. I think Ken Loach has got a lot of guts to film it that way.'

Sunday Mirror film critic Jack Bentley wrote, 'To an extent the makers have excelled themselves in a matter of typecasting ... In real life, when John wasn't in Wandsworth Prison, he was taking on all the toughs on his home ground of Fulham. Many of his pals, who have known him since he was first picked up by the law for malicious damage at the age of eleven, have also been in and out of prison. The star casting of an ex-convict, even with the purpose of achieving authenticity, could still be regarded as yet another publicity gimmick.'

But Bindon took his role in *Poor Cow* very seriously and

Chapter Three

was infuriated by press suggestions that he was just there to make up the numbers. 'This is a chance for me to get away from all the bad stuff for good,' he said at the time. 'I'm going to work my socks off on this role and anyone who suggests otherwise will get a visit from me.' Even away from the shady world of criminality, Bindon couldn't resist a little reference to the past.

After *Poor Cow*, Bindon was almost immediately cast in a forthcoming all-star film called *Inspector Clouseau*, which seemed to put paid to the theory that he was a one-hit wonder, a thug with nowhere to turn. However, many so-called professional actors remained outraged that an untrained former pheasant-plucker may have done them out of a job, and there were probing questions asked about how Bindon got his Equity card. Even members of Bindon's own family joined in the furore – one of Bindon's uncles by marriage was an actor. As cousin Gordon Wilson later explained, 'When Johnny got the part in *Poor Cow* our uncle was quite miffed because he'd got an Equity card the same way as everyone else.'

When the *Sunday Mirror*'s Jack Bentley asked Bindon about the Equity accusations on the set of *Poor Cow*, Bindon just shrugged his shoulders. 'I'd feel like taking a punch at someone if I was an out-of-work actor and I was pipped for a good role by some chap like me. But what would anybody with a record who wants to stay out of jug do when a chance like this comes up?'

However, Bindon was worried about how his new career would be greeted back on his manor. 'It's just that anybody who acts is supposed to be a poof,' he explained to one reporter, 'and, if I get called that, there's gonna be a few more broken heads around. But then most of my pals are layabouts and I owe them nothing but trouble. I don't blame all my trouble on my environment though. I've had this overwhelming urge to smash things since I was a kid. In Fulham every tough wants to take me on! I don't want to fight, but that's all I've ever been inside for. At least if you're a thief there's a chance of getting something for nothing. But thieving doesn't appeal to me. This is the longest I've been out of jug since I was eleven. If I can be a success in films, maybe I'll stay out.'

Bindon was already becoming an adept self-publicist, capable of embellishing the truth by lying about the reasons behind some of his prison sentences. To admit he'd been sent down for living off immoral earnings just didn't have quite the same ring to it.

Poor Cow was eventually sold for a small fortune to an American distributor, but Bindon only received a modest £1,000 fee for his role, worth about £25,000 today. 'It was enough to keep me going for a while, but it wasn't the sort of riches I'd been lead to believe I'd earn,' he explained many years later.

However, a television play called *Profile of a Gentlemen* was looming and Bindon was also rehearsing another TV project called *Thirty Year Stretch*. He admitted at the time, 'All the parts are villains but I'm not afraid of being typecast – after all, Humphrey Bogart was pretty successful and he didn't go helping old ladies across the street very often.'

Bindon was lapping up all the publicity and attention. He was being feted in the trendy end of the King's Road and treated like a film star back on his home turf of Fulham. But real-life dramas were never far away for John Bindon.

Chapter Four

One night in late 1967, Bindon was walking across Putney Bridge after a night in a pub south of the river when he noticed a man hurriedly stripping off his clothes. He couldn't resist asking him what was happening. 'What's all this about then, mate?' The man explained that his best friend had just fallen in the Thames. Bindon peered over the side and could see nothing. As he later explained, 'I figured that, if anybody was in the water, the tide would have carried him to the other side of the bridge.'

Meanwhile, the man who was about to jump in admitted he couldn't swim. 'So I stripped off and sure enough I then spotted this fella in the water on the other side. I dived straight in, 'cos I don't like jumping from heights, and what happens? I hit the bottom. I think I must have hit my head on one of the safes I threw over the bridge in the days when I was a villain.'

The current had immediately sucked him under the water, and he found himself struggling to stay afloat. 'I had a lot of trouble with the current and with this poor bloke, who's not only drowning but, I later found out, had epilepsy, and he's a hell of a handful. Every time I hold him up he fights free and goes under. And then we get caught in a whirlpool and I lose him, and then I nearly get lost myself, and then the cops fish me out. What a comedown, being fished out by the cops!'

Bindon's account given to journalists the following day did little to express the emotional upheaval he felt after failing to save the man in the river. Less than an hour after it had happened, Bindon visited his relatives, the Wilsons, at their home near Putney Bridge. 'He was very upset,' explained cousin Gordon Wilson later, 'because he'd tried to make a grab for the guy. I remember him saying he dived in and it was so murky he couldn't see anything. He was trying to find the guy and then he saw his blue anorak through the mud. He grabbed the anorak and in doing that the bloke pulled out and slipped off into the water. Johnny was upset because he was so close to saving him. It freaked him out badly.'

The Wilsons and Bindons have always been irritated by later stories that implied he had thrown the man into the river in the first place and then tried to turn himself into a hero. 'I saw how upset he was and there's no way Johnny set it up,' insisted Gordon. 'These stories about him are outrageous. He would never do something like that. For God's sake, he dived in to save a man without any consideration for his own safety.'

Fleet Street had a field day reporting Bindon's rescue

Chapter Four

attempt. On 22 October 1968, the London *Evening News* splashed the headline 'Poor Cow star dives 40ft in rescue bid' across their front page. For the first time in her life, Bindon's mum Ciss found herself being interviewed by reporters. A week later, on 5 November 1968, Bindon was praised by Putney coroner Dr John Burton who recorded a verdict of misadventure on the victim, twenty-two-year-old William Hill of Vincent Street, Westminster. The court heard that Bindon had dived in, even though it was pitch dark and misty, and there was a strong tide running at the time. Sergeant Albert Breckton informed the coroner, 'Mr Bindon is going to be put up for a bravery award.' And the coroner himself noted, 'One person who was not concerned in this matter jumped into the water in an attempt to save this man. It was an exceptionally brave act.'

Bindon later received a Queen's Medal for bravery. Typically he couldn't resist turning it all into one big joke when he told reporters, 'When I was a wild young man, I hit an awful lot of people, mostly policemen, who got in my way, when I was having a small tickle. I did most of my time in stir for hitting coppers. And I know it sounds crackers, but it's the coppers who put me up for this medal.' Of his past feud with the police, he added, 'Well, they're all right, I suppose, but I won't have them taking liberties with me. Funny about this medal, isn't it? But then that's life, ain't it?'

Meanwhile, back in the criminal hinterlands of Fulham, trouble was brewing. Bindon's acting roles might have meant a measure of fame on his manor, but it didn't stop certain shady characters wanting to take a pop at the newly crowned 'celebrity' hard man. One of those with a score to settle was a giant of a man called Ginger Chowles, whose family hailed from Paddington. Ginger was a classic professional criminal who had never done an honest day's work in his life. He had a long police record, including serving eighteen months for 'chinning a copper' – a charge he always insisted was a fit-up. As his son Vince recalled many years later, 'My father was a great adversary of Bindon's.'

Trouble between the two men kicked off when they were both drinking in The Star pub behind Bindon's rented mews house in Belgravia. 'There had been a niggle between them for some time,' Vince Chowles recalled, 'and one day my father was drunk and started having a go at Bindon. Then Bindon ran over and kicked him so hard my dad fell down the stairs from the bar and broke his arm. Bindon jumped on top of him and continued hitting him. Eventually a showgirl called Suzie broke up the fight.' Bindon walked away virtually unscathed.

Bindon always insisted Chowles had pressed him for a fight and denied he came close to killing him that night. He even told one friend many years later, 'Ginger was spoiling for a fight. I had no truck with him, but he thought he could take me on so I had no choice but to steam in.'

As Vince Chowles later explained, 'The problem between Bindon and my dad was really tribal stuff. We were from Paddington and he was from Fulham and there was a constant state of war between us all. My old man was a very big guy and he loved to have a fight. But in my opinion Bindon took a liberty that time. Funny thing is that my old man told me years later that if you win and give them a really good hiding they don't come back. Then I asked him if that was why he'd never gone back to Bindon

Chapter Four

and he kind of shrugged. It took my old man quite a long time to get over that hiding.'

Back in Bindon's other world of beautiful people, dolly girls and King's Road fashionistas, his acting career was going from strength to strength. His appearance as a villain in the BBC's *Wednesday Play* brought him into contact with another actor from the wrong side of the tracks, George Sewell, who later recalled that, 'Bindon was great company. One of the funniest men I've ever met in my life. He didn't tell one joke. He just made things very funny. Mind you, he could also be a bloody liability. I was with him in a pub one night when he laid into this guy after they had an argument. The other fella nearly ended up in hospital. We all left rather hurriedly within minutes.'

In the centre of this increasingly bizarre double life was Bindon's lover Sheila Davis. He would spend two or three nights a week at her flat opposite The Britannia, but refused to live with her full-time, preferring his bachelor flophouse in Belgravia and the occasional meal back at his mum and dad's flat in Sullivan Court. Even after Sheila became pregnant with their child and decided that, when the baby was born, she wanted to move back to her old manor of Elephant and Castle, Bindon refused to commit to her full-time. Their daughter Kelly was born in 1967, and Sheila moved back to her tiny council flat with the baby and her three other children from her marriage, as well as her six dogs. She later said that Bindon often did the babysitting for her. 'I used to go out and leave John babysitting with the four kids. I'd come home and find him changing nappies. I'll never forget the day he called me from the Fulham laundry. He was very upset and said,

"Get down here quick, Sheila. Some woman has taken the ironing machine and it's my turn next."'

Years later she recalled, 'We grew apart when John became involved with the film set. I can't stand most of the "Hello, darling!" crowd. But for years we had a very special relationship.' Bindon never hid the truth about Kelly, and his mum Ciss regularly popped over to Elephant and Castle to see her granddaughter. She was saddened that the child never had a proper full-time father, but her son always continued to visit Sheila and Kelly regularly, and tried his hardest to make sure they were never short of cash.

Bindon's determination to make it in the acting game seemed to take priority over everything else, including his girlfriend and child; and Bindon's relatives were in awe of his newfound fame as an actor. Cousin Gordon Wilson remembered, 'The acting side of it seemed cool to me as a kid. It was like an outlet from the criminal world. But then Johnny was very clever and could sit and discuss any subject and be extremely knowledgeable about it. People expected him to be some kind of hardened thug, but he really wasn't like that.' And Bindon made a point of never discussing the heavier aspects of his personal life with close family members. 'He never involved any of us in his problems. He just stuck to telling us the funny incidents, including the habit he had for sticking his twelve-inch willy into people's letterboxes – "just for a laugh"!'

Bindon even told Wilson he had landed another acting gig in which he had to drive a car, although he hadn't bothered telling the producers he couldn't drive. 'I'll manage somehow. They'll never know,' he assured his

Chapter Four

young cousin. Amazingly he pulled it off, and nobody noticed that he wasn't a qualified driver.

One of Bindon's new famous show-business pals was hard-living, hard-drinking actor Richard Harris, who was fascinated by his criminal background. Harris was starring as Oliver Cromwell when he ended up on a marathon drinking session with Bindon in Chelsea. They also took along John Murphy, heir to a building fortune, who was a close friend of Harris. They ended up downing flaming sambucas and got so drunk Harris kept burning the end of his nose. Bindon thought it was hilarious that Harris couldn't film for a week afterwards while his burned nose healed. That same night they chatted up a stunning American woman in a bar and tossed a coin to decide who would sleep with her. Harris got the girl, and for once Bindon had to let his pal bed the beauty. Such was life in the weird and wonderful world of John Bindon.

Bindon and a few of his criminal associates were now regularly mingling with the rich, the louche and the creative who characterised sixties London, so it wasn't that surprising when, in the autumn of 1968, he was recruited to act in one of the most controversial films ever made in Britain. *Performance* promised to highlight the frivolous and easy hedonism of London, which had started to take on darker hues. Many believe this film cast a dark shadow over everyone who took part in it. But the story of how John Bindon and everyone else came together to produce a 'masterpiece' is fascinating.

Young artist-turned-scriptwriter Donald Cammell's screenplay explored the nature of identity – particularly sexual identity – and the idea that the energy of the artist was derived from the same violent source as that of the criminal. It was a potent mix. Bindon got his actual chance in *Performance* thanks to the project's so-called 'technical adviser' David Litvinoff, a mysterious figure who mingled in the worlds of crime, Bohemia and hedonism and knew Bindon from his haunts on the King's Road. Litvinoff's friend George Melly once described him as a man 'who understood entirely the excitement of violence'. Litvinoff flitted between the worlds of the artist and the criminal. He was intimate with the Krays (it was rumoured he had once been Ronnie's lover) and friends with artists Francis Bacon and Lucian Freud.

John Bindon first met Litvinoff at the time of the infamous Redlands drugs bust in 1967, when Mick Jagger, Keith Richards and their friend Robert Fraser were arrested following a police raid on Richards's country house. Jagger ended up spending time in prison after being charged with unauthorised possession of four tablets containing amphetamine sulphate, and there was a lot of anger about who had grassed up the Stones to the police. Litvinoff – who already knew Jagger and the rest of the band – decided to find out who had blown the whistle, and suspicion soon fell on a casual acquaintance of Jagger's. Litvinoff and Bindon visited the unfortunate man and set about beating a confession out of him. 'They gave him a right hammering. He'd broken the golden rule and snitched, so he had to pay the price,' explained one of Bindon's oldest friends many years later. 'John said Jagger was a little freaked out when he heard what had happened, but at least he knew it would never happen again.'

Chapter Four

In *Performance*, Chas – played brilliantly against type by James Fox – is a gangland enforcer, a psychopathic thug who takes sadistic delight in putting the frighteners on car-hire firms and bookmakers. On the run from the law and his former associates, he takes refuge in the basement flat of the crumbling Notting Hill home of a rock star called Turner, played by Mick Jagger. Turner has long since lost the plot, and spends much of his time with two bisexual female companions in a listless round of drugs and sex. In Chas, he recognises the 'demon' he has lost himself. Turner and his strange companions start to break down Chas's identity in a crucible of sexuality and hallucinogenic drugs. Weird sex and bloody violence eventually dominate the proceedings.

Bindon and Litvinoff eventually used their own real-life experiences as the basis for some of the most violent scenes in *Performance*. These include the moment when criminal Chas brutally shaves the head of a chauffeur. This was filmed in the lock-up garage next to Bindon's home in Chesham Mews and ended with him and other villains covering another criminal's Rolls-Royce with acid. At one stage, Chas threatens Bindon's character Moody when he won't stop talking during a bloodthirsty torture scene. The look of contempt on Bindon's face says it all when he looks towards Fox's character. 'We all knew then that John had been there in real life,' said Billy Murray, who also had a small part in *Performance*. Litvinoff and Bindon even arranged for Fox to visit the Thomas A Beckett boxers' pub in the Old Kent Road to get a taste of what it was like to be 'one of the chaps'.

During the filming of *Performance*, Bindon's intake of

hashish increased significantly, which undoubtedly heightened the prevailing air of unreality surrounding many scenes in the film. Co-star Anita Pallenberg later admitted taking heroin supplied to her on surreptitious visits to the set from her dealer 'Spanish' Tony Sanchez. These days Anita Pallenberg looks back on *Performance* as 'the end of the beautiful sixties – the end of love and all that'.

In the middle of filming, Bindon went on a pub crawl with some of his co-stars and ended up having three punch-ups in various pubs. One actor said afterwards, 'It was like a living nightmare. John might have been used to such real-life violence, but it terrified the rest of us.' Next morning, he arrived on set looking very happy with himself. Billy Murray takes up the story: 'John had this matchbox in his hand which he kept shaking around. Then he asked me, "D'you want to know what's in it." I said, "No, John." There was a thumb in it. Some guy had stuck his finger in Bindon's mouth during one of the fights and he'd bitten it off at the top joint and it was still in the matchbox.'

Bindon chuckled gently as he told Murray and other horrified cast members about the thumb. 'The guy's been calling my mum all night. He wants it back. Reckons the hospital could sew it back on, but I'm not going to give it back to him.' Yet again, he had wheeled out the old chestnut he had been using to amuse himself and his pals since he was a kid. No one ever asked to see the so-called 'thumb' close-up, so the legend continued to grow.

Towards the end of *Performance*, James Fox's character Chas – his mind blown to smithereens by Turner, the girls and the mushrooms – imagines a short-haired, business-

Chapter Four

suited Turner at the office desk of his boss Harry Flowers, and the gang start swaying and stripping to Stones-type rock music. There had been no advance warning of this in the script, and Bindon was one of only two actors who agreed to strip off on camera. One of the actors on set at the time said, 'Bindon had no inhibitions at all. In fact, he was rather chuffed to be asked to strip naked, and he naturally made a point of ensuring all of us saw his vast manhood swinging around like a third leg.'

After the completion of *Performance*, David Litvinoff started to find his shady past catching up with him. He retreated to Wales, then later to Australia, before returning to London an unhappy man. 'He didn't want to be old,' recalled one friend. 'He didn't even want to be middle-aged.' Litvinoff eventually killed himself with an overdose of sleeping pills, aged forty-six.

Performance was eventually released after being heavily censored by Warner Brothers and the British Board of Film Censors. But, as film critic Derek Malcolm pointed out at the time, 'It is a violent movie, it is a movie which is frank about sex and, above all, it is a movie which admits and explores the correlation between sex and violence and power. It constantly reiterates some shocking things. But what it does not do is approve of them.' Bindon had accidentally found himself starring in a film that still stands to this day as the quintessential record of sixties London – a London of hedonism, amorality and violence – with its exploration of sexuality, the mind-bending properties of hallucinogenic drugs and the meeting of the worlds of pop music and crime. Bindon admitted that the film left an indelible mark of him.

Part of the legend of *Performance* is that it is the film that drove James Fox first to a breakdown, and then to God. This is not true, although Fox – who regards the film as a masterpiece – chose not work for ten years after completing it.

There was one aspect of acting which John Bindon could not get his head around: auditions. He hated them, especially when he didn't get the parts. If that happened, he would usually grit his teeth and try to grin and bear it before going home and punching a few holes in the wall, or going out and getting slaughtered before picking a fight with somebody who no doubt deserved it.

On one occasion, a skinny, Oxbridge-educated movie director got right up Bindon's nose by telling him his teeth needed fixing and that he should attend auditions in a suit. 'You fuckin' what?' bellowed Bindon at the director.

'Your appearance is crucial to me and, quite frankly, you look a bloody awful mess …'

The director didn't know what was about to hit him. 'I'm not yer fuckin' toy boy,' screamed Bindon. 'I got a job humping crates in between acting jobs, and you're telling me to wear a suit. Why don't you fuck off!'

With that, Bindon lunged towards the director, who turned and ran towards the casting agent at the back of the hall. Bindon picked up speed, then looked at all the other actors and realised he was the centre of attention so he stopped, kicked a chair into the air and stormed out. Years later, he met the same director at a posh cocktail party in Knightsbridge. The man immediately fled the house with Bindon laughing out loud. 'Fuckin' prat!'

Chapter Four

The whole point was that Bindon's chipped teeth and rough appearance worked entirely to his advantage most of the time, as he was usually cast as a criminal or so-called bad boy. But he genuinely believed that more demanding acting roles and greater recognition were only just around the corner. For the first time in his life he was actually feeling relatively good about himself, and was happy with the way his career seemed to be going. He wasn't earning great fortunes – his mum still fed him most days – but there was enough cash in the kitty for him to keep up his all-important social life, where strings were pulled and a chance meeting could make the difference between holes in your shoes and a major movie role. He knew the film business was incestuous, and that who you knew – or drank with, or slept with – often played a bigger role in acting success than what you were capable of.

But the cold, hard world of London criminality was never far away. In late 1969, Detective Chief Superintendent Terence O'Connell was investigating the murder of a notorious gambler called Mickey Harris who had been gunned down outside Toby's Club in Tower Bridge Road. O'Connell paid a routine visit to Bindon's lover Sheila Davis, who was by now living in Louise House, Blendon Row in Walworth, south London. She told him she believed a shooting war was on the verge of erupting between rival gangs in the East Street Market area of Walworth.

Bindon became involved in the feud when a Scotsman jabbed Sheila in the face with a glass at a party after hearing she had been talking to the police. Not surprisingly, Bindon took up the cudgels on her behalf, and more or less damned all Scotsmen. He was on the warpath, so, when Hugh Mailon Brannon, a thirty-two-year-old bricklayer from east London, admitted that he knew the perpetrator, Bindon attacked him and Brannon received severe throat injuries. He was later fined for causing Brannon actual bodily harm. But following that assault, Brannon swore revenge and, on 3 November 1969, Brannon and Patrick McLaughlin, another bricklayer, barged into Sheila Davis's flat and demanded to know where Bindon was. Brannon yelled at her, 'He's going to get this,' and flashed a gun in a shoulder holster tucked under his coat. At the Old Bailey, both Brannon and McLaughlin later admitted visiting Sheila Davis at her flat, but denied that they were armed. They insisted the police had falsified evidence against them. The jury eventually found both men guilty by a majority verdict, and Brannon was jailed for five years for intent to commit a felony, possessing a firearm and possessing ammunition. McLaughlin was found guilty of possessing a firearm with intent to commit a felony and jailed for eighteen months.

Over in Sheila's street an uneasy peace reigned. One Glasgow-born detective described the area as 'worse than the Gorbals', with an almost daily series of stabbings, wife-beatings and closing-time brawls. Fear of gang terror, which had caused many families to leave the area, was rife.

One person who, thanks to John Bindon, ended up inhabiting an uneasy grey area between criminality and show business was a musician called John Porter, who befriended him in the early 1970s through the King's Road set. 'I would just say Bindon was a great person. My main recollection of him was that he was always laughing. John

Chapter Four

compartmentalised his life very carefully most of the time, but he did let his guard down.'

At the time, Porter was a guitarist with Brian Ferry's Roxy Music. This university-educated, grammar-school boy had been brought up by Catholic Jesuit priests, which led to heavy conversations about Catholicism with Bindon. 'I had a place in Roland Gardens next door to Blakes Hotel at the time. He just started turning up at any time of the night or day, but he was one of the few people I didn't mind turning up. He was always great value. He admitted to me that he never told any of his criminal pals he was coming to my place because he liked to have a bolthole they didn't know about. At the start of our friendship he was quite careful about not allowing the two worlds to mix. He'd turn up after a fight in a pub or whatever. We'd sit up for days talking, smoking pot – which seemed to calm him down – and playing endless games of Scrabble. We talked about everything.'

At first, Bindon made it clear he didn't want Porter anywhere near his criminal associates. 'He mentioned how people got their arms sawed off and stuff like that. Many of my friends in the music business couldn't handle him. They were kind of scared of him, but I never judged him. I think that was the key to our friendship.'

Despite needing the occasional puff on a joint to calm his temper, Bindon and virtually all his criminal associates were fiercely anti-drugs at the time. 'The crims were scared of drugs back then. They used to call people like me "fuckin' druggies". Bindon was so locked into his criminal life and territory that any relationship – including my friendship with him – was very intense.'

However, Bindon began revealing an altogether different side to his character when he was with John Porter. 'He was very critical about certain other people who he felt weren't genuine. He had an opinion about everything and when I put some Hank Williams music on he fell in love with it.' The two men began going to music concerts together, including at least two London appearances by guitarist Ry Cooder. Porter gave Bindon a small Jamaican guitar that he used to strum along to whatever record was on the turntable. 'He'd roll his eyes and strum away like a naughty little boy,' recalls Porter. Bindon particularly liked Woody Guthrie, as well as black blues music. He told Porter he identified with black people because he had always felt like an outsider. At one stage Bindon was close to tears as he confessed to Porter that he believed he had never got any really big acting roles because of his working-class background. 'He said it was an uphill struggle to get work and he wasn't sure he would ever really make it.

'Bindon had this magnetic effect on people. He knew it, but ended up exploiting it half the time, and the other half trying to escape it. He told me that when he was at school people often made fun of him. He didn't know where he belonged. We used to call his mews home the siege house because it was the place where he used to often go to escape from the pressures of life. But you know, I think he was quite a romantic person, and he was certainly very creative, but found it difficult to express that.'

Bindon surprised Porter by showing a deep knowledge of literature – Porter, of course, was unaware that Dennis Bindon had always encouraged his children to read and educate themselves. 'We had a lot of authors in common

Chapter Four

and I remember giving him a book by an intellectual travel writer called Paddy Lee Firmer about how he left home in Holland and walked to Transylvania in the thirties. I passed it on to John and we talked quite a lot about it. He had a very good take on it. We also both liked reading Evelyn Waugh and also John Marshall, who wrote about people and places in India. He'd remember great chunks of books that we'd read. No wonder he was good at remembering lines.' Bindon also told Porter he was an avid reader of military campaigns. 'He loved Wellington and all that kind of stuff, and he felt that in different circumstances he would have been an incredible soldier.

'When John walked into a room he filled it up. I think right from early on when I met him there was a lot of what I'd call intelligent, sharp reflection. He was trying to deal with these frustrations. I never pried into what had happened in his life. If he wanted help, I would be there for him.'

As their friendship progressed, Bindon became more and more open about his criminal connections. 'It was all about trust with John, and once he was certain I was on his side and not judgemental, then he felt more confident about letting me into that other side of his life.'

Bindon started taking long-haired hippy Porter to criminal clubs in west London. 'On a few occasions we'd leave somewhere because John wanted to avoid trouble. He'd also introduce me to some very heavy-looking characters. It was like living in a Damon Runyan scenario. Harry the Helmet and Seldom Seen Kid. Many of these people had strange nicknames and squashed noses.'

One time, Bindon travelled down to stay with Porter at

a castle he had rented in Dorset. 'It was an amazing weekend. Some people I knew were astonished I could spend a weekend in Dorset with crazy John Bindon. But he was such a laugh and my lasting memory of him was with a blanket over his shoulders tearing across the moor. Complete lunatic. A big fucking teddy bear.'

Eventually Bindon began turning up at Porter's apartment with a few strange faces. 'Often these people were completely disarmed by me. They saw me as some druggie, hippy musician – which I was, really. John would take the piss out of them, and later we'd laugh about all of them. He just brought them round so we could get off on the madness of it all.'

On one occasion, Bindon and Porter went to a party at the trendy end of the Portobello Road. 'There were a couple of well-known rock stars and it was packed, so we sat down against a wall opposite the front door. Then the police turned up and there was a bag filled with drugs on a coffee table in the middle of the floor. John just calmly got up and bundled the police out on to the street. He came back twenty minutes later having sorted it all out.'

A few days later, Bindon turned up once again at Porter's flat in the middle of the night. 'John was with this heavy guy who was sweating and very ill at ease and shifty. John took me into the kitchen and said this guy was in bad shape and he was public enemy number one and there was nowhere else in the world that he could be left. It was awful. You could see a gun sticking out of this man's trousers. He wouldn't sit down and he was pacing around, and because my wife was there it made it even more difficult.' Even worse was the fact that Porter had just dropped a tab of

Chapter Four

acid, so he decided to come clean to Bindon and his criminal associate. 'This fella already thought we were freaks, so I said, "To be honest with you, I've taken this drug and I can't reverse the situation. Sorry, but that's the way it is, but it makes you feel really good." There was a confrontation at first and I thought the guy was going to pull his gun on me, but then he calmed down.'

Porter then offered the acid to Bindon's criminal friend, assuring him that it might make him feel better. 'The guy reluctantly said OK, so I gave him some. Then, within twenty minutes, he started to groan. I was sitting there. My wife was hiding in the bedroom and suddenly he says, "Where have I been all my life?" This guy eventually became a very good friend and I met him many times over the following year. His name was Dave and he never used to knock on my front door. He'd just come in and out through an open window. He told me he felt safer that way because the police were after him throughout this period.'

Porter later concluded that his life with Bindon was like a real-life version of *Performance*. 'John kept banging on about how realistic *Performance* was. The trouble was that, if we were ever in a pub and someone gave me a hard time, he'd always want to beat them up and I had to hold him back. John thrived on the drama, but ultimately became a victim of it. There was always this rueful inevitability about John. He knew he was very capable, strong, sharp-minded and pretty intelligent with this incredible capacity for memory. But there was also much tragedy behind that ever-present smile. I think all the inevitability of his life had already kicked in.'

Chapter Five

Back in 1963, Victoria Alexandra Hodge, daughter of Sir John and Lady Hodge, had donned Mummy's pearls and a cheesy smile before attending a debs' ball. She had grown up with homes in Surrey and Sussex along with her two sisters. Cut to five years later and you have Vicki Hodge '68 style, with long blonde hair and a silver micromini. 'I grew three inches, lost four pounds, peeled off those ghastly black fur eyelashes, washed off a ton of pink-and-white powder and grew that diabolical hair.'

Vicki's family motto was 'Glory is the Reward of Virtue'. 'I didn't think that when they decided on it they could have had me in mind,' she admitted. She was born on 17 October 1946 and attended twelve schools as the family moved around the world. Aged sixteen, on holiday in Italy, she walked into a smart Florentine fashion salon and announced, 'I'm a top British model.' They gave her a job.

She subsequently became the lover of society photographer David Bailey.

Vicki – by now a six-guinea-an-hour model – explained, 'First I went through a Beat period – turned up for work in nothing but a body stocking and a six-foot wig. People stopped booking me because I was "too kinky". I had to pull myself together and learn to dress like a real live girl.'

Vicki Hodge's take on life is summed up neatly in her own words: 'Never refuse in this job or you don't work. If they ask whether you can skydive, walk the tightrope or jump through flaming hoops in a mink bikini, you say, "Sure, I've done it dozens of times." There wasn't anything I wouldn't do for a great glamour shot. I've done it all myself without the benefit of publicity men – with just my own exhibitionism. Contrary to the public's idea of a model, I've never been told I had to lie on my back. As for the future, I can only hope that something else turns up when my fun bags lose their appeal.' On the subject of men she said, 'Men are like buses. If you miss one there is another just around the corner.' And of her former friends in the aristocracy she said, 'They think because I appear in newspapers in my pants and bra that I am below contempt.'

But Vicki Hodge adored the King's Road-style life. She boasted to friends about owning 400 pairs of shoes and 100 pairs of boots. She also claimed in one interview to have lifted the British mini-skirt to a record height – six inches above her handbag – by 'buying Marks & Spencer kilts for seven-year-olds'.

Vicki walked into Bindon's life when they were both appearing in a Marty Feldman film called *Every Home Should Have One*. As Vicki later explained, 'I'd never seen

Chapter Five

the like of him before – a huge, handsome, 100 per cent man. I thought, God, what a hulk, and started chatting him up.' Vicki even wrote messages on Bindon's arm in biro: 'Will you marry me?', 'Will you make love to me?' As she looked at his enormous hands she realised he had obviously recently had a fight because all the knuckles were dislodged.

Three weeks later Bindon and Vicki had their first dinner date, and she explained to him that she was about to get married to wealthy advertising executive and Old Harrovian Ian Heath. Vicki told Bindon that, although she was earning good money as a top model, she desperately wanted the security that marriage could provide, and it would enable her to give up the job. She later insisted that nothing happened between Bindon and her that night. But their next date started with a boozy lunch with actor Richard Harris and his brother Dermot. Afterwards they all went back to Harris's flat. John and Vicki could hardly take their hands off each other, and they ended up in Richard Harris's elegant bedroom complete with a massive double bed and flowing curtains. 'The force between John and me was so strong that within ten minutes we were in the bedroom ... with Richard and Dermot singing Irish songs outside the door. It was the most fabulous love session of my life, everything love should be. After that day we made perfect love whenever we could.'

Bindon later summed up his relationship with Vicki Hodge when he confessed, 'All that womanising ended when I met Vicki. Well, almost all! She was knockout beautiful and an exhibitionist like me. We were crazy about each other but she was due to marry this chinless wonder.'

When Ian Heath got wind of a problem just a few days before their high-society wedding, Vicki convinced him that her love for Bindon was over. 'I was foolish to believe her,' he later admitted. However, Vicki went ahead with the wedding party because her husband's parents had promised the couple a home in Chelsea. She even spent part of her pre-wedding night with Bindon at the Grosvenor House Hotel. And, as she walked out into the December sunshine following the marriage ceremony, there was Bindon, his eyes full of tears, watching from across the street. Choking back her own tears, Vicki climbed into a waiting Bentley with her new husband. The car then wound its way down to Hyde Park Corner before heading along Bindon's beloved King's Road. Just then, Vicki turned to find Bindon driving a Mini alongside her in a traffic jam just west of Sloane Square.

At Vicki's Chelsea wedding reception later that afternoon were actor George Lazenby, model Sandra Paul (now wife of Tory politician Michael Howard), artist James Gilroy and furrier Charles Blane, who gave Vicki a three-foot-long silver-fox wrap. After less than an hour, she slipped away from her new husband on the pretext of going to the hairdresser. She walked down the road to Bindon's favourite pub, The Britannia. Moments later, the couple slipped across the street to a friend's flat and made love.

For many months, Bindon waited outside Vicki's posh house in Seymour Walk, just off Fulham Road, which she shared with her new husband. 'I used to wait until Ian had gone to bed,' she later explained, 'and then run out to John. I would be cooking six meals a day, starting with breakfast for Ian and then breakfast for John. He may have

Chapter Five

come from a different background to me, but we got on fabulously. Some people in my family tried to put him down, but he was the best man I have ever had a relationship with. I know he had affairs with other women, and I hated him for it. We had rows over it, of course, but he always returned to me. There would be nobody else.'

And at The Britannia, landlady Nora Hayes was well aware that Bindon was playing with fire. 'Look, we saw them going off together after the wedding and they were in here virtually every bloody night after she got married. Vicki was all right. I'll give her her due because she never landed us in it and we used to get a lot of problems with the police.'

Years later, Vicki claimed Bindon had encouraged her to marry Heath. 'I could never give you anything like that,' he told her. 'I have no money. You must marry Ian.' There is no doubt Bindon could not offer Vicki the stable life she yearned for, so she remained married for the time being; but the pattern of her married life consisted of counting the hours until she could be with her lover. Vicki and Bindon were so besotted with each other they made love 'ten times a day' in public places such as the subway on Hyde Park Corner and the alleyway round the corner from her home. They also had sex in their friends' flats, in lifts, in the back of taxis and in her car. Sometimes they would go to a boring movie and make love in a deserted back row while a friend sat in front keeping guard.

Bindon and Richard Harris were set to star together in a film called *Man in the Wilderness* which was later described as 'a costly and time-wasting partnership'. In

Man in the Wilderness, Harris played a Canadian fur-trapper who survives a mauling by a grizzly bear and then sets out for revenge. Bindon arrived on location in Spain with a contract promising him third billing. The legendary actor-director John Huston was also starring, so it promised to be a tinderbox scenario.

Harris and Bindon immediately began sharing their off-set hours in Spain together. On his first night, Bindon celebrated by getting so drunk he had to be escorted back to his hotel room by police after he threatened to smash up a local bar. Then filming had to be halted to allow the healing of cuts and bruises Harris and Bindon had suffered in a drunken brawl that ended with a punch-up in a dusty ditch. Director Richard Sarafian decided Bindon had to be fired. A hastily convened script conference resulted in Bindon's 'premature and suitably painful' screen death. 'They killed him off with a spear through the back. They just couldn't handle John off set,' recalled Vicki.

Despite this setback, Bindon and Harris remained friends and would invariably meet to celebrate St Patrick's Day. Bindon also linked up in Chelsea with Harris just a few days after Harris had embarked on one of the biggest drinking benders of all time following divorce from his wife Elizabeth. That also ended in a punch-up. Not long afterwards, Harris was the guest on a TV talk show in which viewers were encouraged to ring in. All of a sudden a very broad Glaswegian accent came on the line. Harris looked at the camera and smiled: he knew it was Bindon who was extremely adept at mimicking accents. Cousin Gordon Wilson, who was watching, explained, 'We knew it was John, but no one else did. It was very funny – he was

Top: Bindon was born and brought up on the 1st floor of this small terraced house close to the Thames, in Fulham. He attended Henry Compton secondary modern in Fulham (*bottom*) and stunned his classmates by climbing to the top of the clocktower and ringing the bell.

Top: Bindon seduced many women, hid numerous fugitives and even encountered MI5 the tiny Belgravia mews house where he lived for many years.

Above: The Gasworks club, just off the New Kings Road, was frequented by everyone from gangsters to members of the Royal Family.

The Star Tavern was just around the corner from Bindon's mews house and he had numerous 'straighteners' in the bar and even encountered one deadly rival there.

Top: Bindon even managed to get a photograph taken of his injuries just weeks after the Darke killing which ended up being splashed across many newspapers.

Above: Bindon's high profile murder trial provoked headlines across the world, but this cartoon in the *Evening Standard* sums up the almost light-hearted attitude shown towards the charges.

Top left: Bindon's great Fulham pal Alan Stanton was a professional criminal who helped Bindon in his battles with many west London drug dealers.

Top right: South London police detective Terry Babbidge was delighted when Bindon killed John Darke, dubbed an evil, two-timing police grass.

Above left: The now derelict Ranelagh Yacht Club was the hole-in-the-wall drinking establishment where Bindon killed the notorious John Darke. Chief Superintendent George Mould (*above right*) led the hunt for Bindon, and also crossed swords with MI5 officers keen to ensure Bindon's links with Princess Margaret were not publicly revealed.

Top: Roxy Music band member John Porter was close to Bindon during the '70s and even sheltered a criminal pal of Bindon's.

Bottom: Bindon's old Fulham pal John Atkins enjoyed many wild nights out and lived to tell the tale.

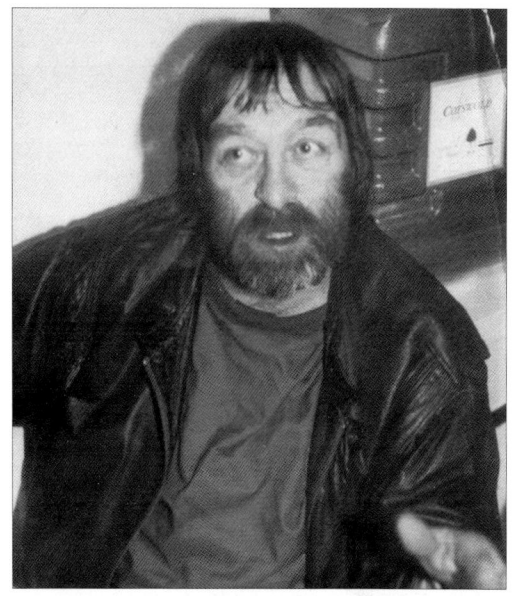

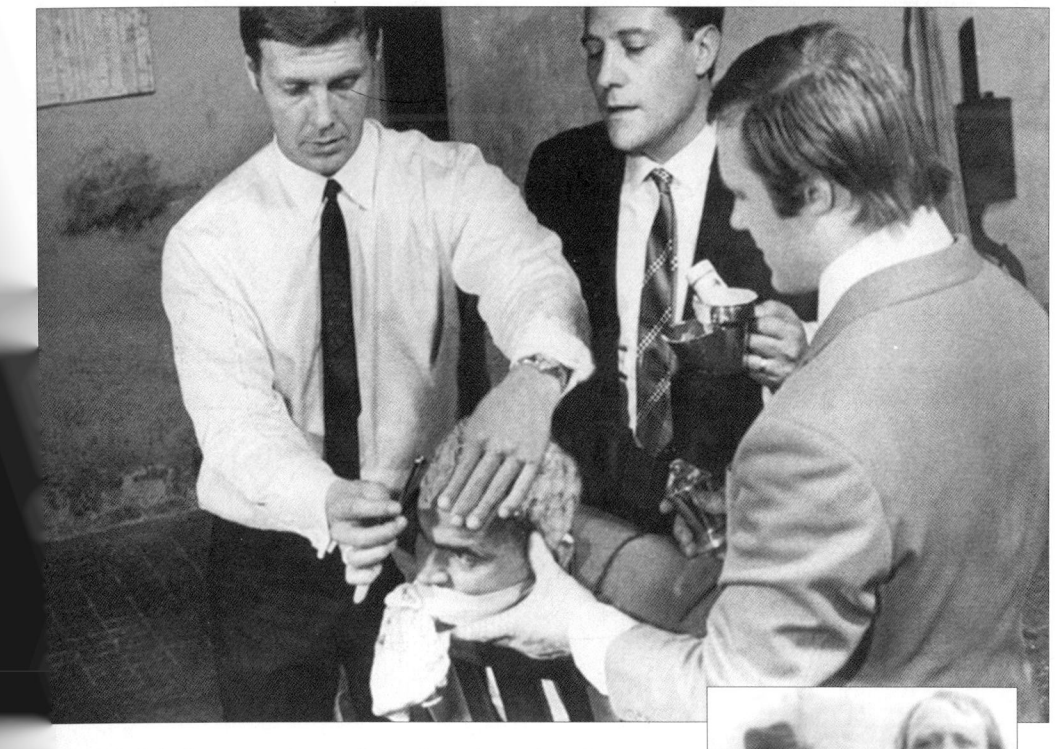

Top left: Bindon was a superb cook and, as the picture shows, even did the washing up afterwards! His brother Mickey (*top right*) was a completely different cup of tea: an unassuming man with a fondness for alcohol who avoided confrontation or attention.

Bottom: The brutal torture scene in *Performance* was closely based on a real-life incident involving Bindon some months earlier. (*Inset*) Bindon loved to play the clown on movie sets and here he is pointing the finger.

Top: Bindon (*left*) with two of the 'chaps' and Roy Dennis, (*far right*) whose clash with John Darke sparked Darke's killing.

Bottom: Bindon was the life and soul of every party he went to.

Chapter Five

asking him questions and the interviewer didn't have a clue it was a set-up job.'

But after Vicki's marriage to Ian Heath, a darker side of Bindon began to emerge. Vicki had become in many ways a gangster's moll. She met members of the Richardson and Kray gangs, and she even saw people stabbed as well as hearing people scream. She had been introduced to a world of extreme violence, but was prepared to be a part of it just to be with Bindon. That violence had an inevitable knock-on effect: when Vicki accused Bindon of being afraid of his father, he picked her up by her ankles and dangled her over the balcony of the fourth-floor flat at Sullivan Court.

Years later, she tried to examine the reasons why she was so besotted with Bindon. She concluded that his violence didn't bother her as much as his infidelity. It also dawned on her that he was a virtual sex addict, capable of two-timing her with anyone who took his fancy. When she suspected that of happening, she would follow him to a block of flats and surprise him while he was in bed with another girl. Vicki would give the couple a right mouthful before racing off as Bindon struggled to get into his clothes. He would then dash into the street after her while Vicki remained in hiding near the flat, before sneaking back into the bedroom of the flat and whacking her opposition squarely on the chin.

Many of Bindon's oldest pals say that he told Vicki about his sexual conquests because he wanted her to back off and stop trying to turn their relationship into something more serious. 'That was John's way. He didn't want Vicki to rely on him in any way because he didn't feel he was entirely worthy of her,' explained one friend.

In the middle of all this, Bindon claimed he had a one-night stand with one of Britain's most famous actresses. He also claimed to have become a close friend of feminist icon Germaine Greer. He told Vicki that Greer noticed he had dirty fingernails and made him wash his hands. Bindon was immensely proud of this alleged friendship. In addition, he seduced a mother and daughter who were one of Vicki's wealthy neighbours. He proudly showed Vicki a note the mother had sent him saying what a great night they had had. He said the two women plied him with alcohol and marijuana and then gave him money and clothes. Another time, Vicki caught Bindon in a pub with a girl and she hit him over the head with a wine carafe. Then she spotted him with yet another woman and drove her car straight through the window of the Chinese restaurant where they were dining. 'Until John, I didn't know I could get so angry, react so wildly, be so violent,' she explained, 'but he brought all that out in me. I was hopelessly, madly in love with him.'

Vicki even tried coping with his infidelity by finding lovers of her own. 'I usually selected the richest man I could, with the biggest car. It was a way of going back to my roots, finding solace with men who understood where I came from and offered me safety and security.' During one break in her relationship with Bindon she dated Hollywood star Elliott Gould: they drove around London for ten days and nights in a white Rolls-Royce and practically lived at the swish Savoy Hotel. 'Elliott was a good, gentle lover. I needed him very much at the time and I don't regret my affair with him.'

Journalist Gordon McGill met Vicki when she agreed to be interviewed for a *Sunday Mirror* feature on modelling in

Chapter Five

1971. 'There was no sign of her husband, but Bindon appeared out of nowhere,' recalled McGill. The three of them set off for a luxury hotel in Sussex for the interview and a photo session. 'Bindon was introduced to me as just John, nothing else. He was like the minder, but I found him very charismatic. He had a presence to him. Even his silence seemed to prove how confident he was of himself. He seemed to know about everything that was going on.'

It was only a few weeks later, when everyone was back in London, that McGill encountered a different side to the couple. 'Vicki turned up at my house one day in tears. She said she couldn't handle being with John any more because of all the guns and violence. I thought she was being a drama queen back then because I had no idea Bindon really was up to no good. She kept saying, "What have I got myself into? I must be crazy to love this man." I knew then she'd got herself mixed up with a very dangerous man.'

McGill believes that Bindon's mixed fortunes perfectly reflected the changes on his home manor of Fulham. 'The area had gone from being purely working class to being gentrified. Lords and ladies were buying up the houses. They were changing the names of the pubs from The Red Lion to the Frog and Whatever. It must have bothered Bindon. Times were changing and I'm not sure he ever fully acknowledged that.'

A few months later, Vicki's marriage to Ian Heath finally collapsed. He gave her enough money to buy a flat opposite Bishop's Park in Fulham, and Bindon – who still lived in that mews house in Belgravia – started spending weeks at a time at Vicki's new home. She even decided she wanted a child and stopped taking the pill, and for a while the relationship seemed to flourish. Bindon and Vicki made a handsome couple and they could now be open about their relationship. He loved being seen around town with beautiful, sexy Vicki, but the old mischief-making Fulham boy was never far from the surface. He still liked shocking people by flashing his twelve-inch penis at people in pubs. Once he even exposed himself in front of eccentric peer Lord Longford, who was then engaged in carrying out a much-celebrated investigation into pornography.

One night, shortly after Vicki's separation from her husband, the couple attended a champagne party at The Star, which backed onto his Belgravia mews house. Bindon's big enemy and love rival George Wright wandered in with another notorious south-London criminal, plus three or four heavy-looking characters. 'They said hello to Vicki,' Bindon later recalled, 'and I was introduced to them. I asked them what they wanted to drink. They said they wanted champagne and I bought a bottle. One of them then grabbed me by the lapels and a fight ensued. They were trying to get me to kneel down so they could pop me. I was threatened and told that if I did not mend my ways I would end up dead. This threat was very much over my relationship with Vicki.'

Bindon said that a mystery man – only ever referred to as Mr X – eventually called off the attackers after a friend of Vicki's intervened and threatened to call the police. George Wright died shortly afterwards, but now it was clear that Bindon's relationship with Vicki had completely spilled over into his criminal activities. A few months later, Vicki got another even more chilling taste of her lover's other life when they were out shopping together in her Mini Cooper

Chapter Five

on the King's Road. Bindon was on a day off from filming *Get Carter* with Michael Caine. His role in the movie was relatively small, although the film was later acclaimed as one of the top British gangster movies ever made.

Suddenly, Bindon pulled a huge sheath knife from inside his cowboy boot and sat with it glistening in the sunlight on his lap. Vicki said nothing as he barked at her to drive him over to some flats in 'severe south London'. He didn't explain why, and she didn't ask. After directing her to a spot in a rundown housing estate, he told her, 'Reverse into that parking space, put your lights off and wait.' It was only then that Vicki realised why, a few hours earlier, Bindon had been testing all the knives in her kitchen drawer at home. Sitting next to her in the mini, he stroked the knife and then turned towards her. 'This one's perfect because it's got a handle that stops your hand going over on to the blade when you stick someone.' Then he calmly slipped the knife back into his cowboy boot and got out of the car. 'Won't be long, babes' were his parting words.

Vicki noticed her hands shaking even though it was midsummer. She stayed glued to her seat. After ten minutes she considered getting out of there, but changed her mind because she didn't want to let Bindon down.

Another ten minutes passed before he came running back and jumped into the car, still carrying the knife, which was now covered in blood. Neither said a word. Vicki started up the car and they headed back to the King's Road. She claimed that Bindon later told her he had cut a man's arm off. She was now party to his criminal activities, but with a man like Bindon it simply went with the territory.

Back in the more upmarket King's Road, Bindon became

close friends with a trendy shoe designer called Terry de Havilland. Today his memories of hanging out with Bindon are vivid, 'despite the fact I was dropping tons of acid at the time'.

De Havilland first met Bindon at a West End nightclub called The Last Resort, which was a regular haunt for pop stars from David Bowie to Paul McCartney. 'I was leaving the club with a whole bunch of celebrity friends, including Bowie, when my girlfriend's mate was shouted at by a local thug. Next thing I know he's given her a push, so I had a right go at him. Suddenly this other really heavy-looking fella is steaming into me and trying to kick me to shit. My trousers split in two and I ended up with twenty-two stitches in my face.'

The same man – John Bindon – turned up at de Havilland's shop on the corner of the King's Road and Beaufort Street the next day. De Havilland was terrified he was about to get another beating. 'But all he wanted to know was what I was going to do about it. I'd just come out of hospital and here I was facing up to the same bastard who'd nearly ripped my face off. I knew the Old Bill were after him because they had his name after he'd left his coat behind in the club.' For a split second de Havilland considered what he was going to do. Then he told Bindon, 'Where I come from in Essex, you don't grass up yer own.'

Bindon thanked his victim and then insisted, 'You know it was nothing to do with me. I just had to help out me mate Johnny.'

De Havilland believes to this day that if he'd been 'some rich boy from Sloane Square' then Bindon might have finished him off there and then. 'Instead, we went over the

Chapter Five

road and had a drink in my local pub, The Roebuck. Bindon was very funny and I liked him instantly. Within a couple of pints, he had even flashed his twelve-inch "wendal" at a couple of annoying mincing poofs. There was never a dull moment with Bindon. He just pulled it out and stuck it through three or four pint mugs and then said to them, "Is this any good for you?" Bindon was like a pig in shit. He was on his own territory and in his element. In many ways I suppose he was untouchable that day.'

De Havilland and Bindon became close friends, and the young cockney shoe designer loved watching him hold court. 'He engaged everyone around him. He had the best bunny [talk] I ever heard. He'd say to women they were "receiving swollen goods" and all that type of thing, and they loved it. None of that political correctness bollocks you get these days.'

Although he was officially dating Vicki Hodge at the time, Bindon still spent many booze- and bird-filled nights back at the tiny house in Chesham Mews. One of de Havilland's girlfriends — a French woman who slept with Bindon — even christened his penis 'Le Pink Helicopter'. 'Visiting Bindon in that house was always filled with craziness,' recalled de Havilland. 'To start with he only had a loo and no bathroom. But we were soon entertaining all sorts of models and other gorgeous birds there. All the beautiful people seemed to be gravitating towards us.'

De Havilland's take on that era is worth hearing: 'It was buzzing back then. Led Zeppelin had their offices just down the road from my shop. The Water Rat, The Man in the Moon and The Roebuck were the three main pubs in the area. On Saturdays all the early punks and the skinheads used to clash in the street outside the shop. One time I was outside The Rat with some of the Led Zeppelin crew and all these kids came up and accused us of being straights, so we all slung our beer all over them. We'd never been called a straight in our lives. It was bloody outrageous and John Bindon gave them plenty of verbal!'

The two men shared many lovers, including a female sporting legend who happily agreed to a threesome with them. 'We called it bookends back in them days. But, hey, if they're up for it – why not? We used to bonk new girls virtually every day. Some of them are very respectable people these days, married to senior politicians, famous in their own right. I sometimes see them on the telly and wonder if their old man knows what they got up to back in those wild days in Chesham Mews.'

De Havilland was on a roll work-wise at the time and paid for all the drinks when he was out with Bindon. 'I used to take Bindon to restaurants and clubs. There was one in Paulson Square where some very famous people hung out.' That's where Bindon first met the larger-than-life Led Zeppelin manager Peter Grant. One music-business insider summed him up: 'Peter Grant was someone you did not fuck with. He was a madman.'

Grant – weighing in at around twenty-five stone – was certainly a memorable figure. People who failed to take him seriously did so at their own peril. On one occasion he got literally stuck in the lavatory at The Water Rat while taking a line of cocaine, and Bindon had to be sent in to dismantle the door and wall of the cubicle so he could be released. 'Bindon ended up ripping everything off its hinges to get Grant out. The whole place got trashed by us that

Chapter Five

day,' recalled de Havilland. Bindon saw himself in Grant. Both men were hard nuts from the wrong side of the track, and they both knew the rules of the street: strike first before you get thumped, don't trust a soul and take every penny you can get because there might not be another job on the horizon.

Bindon still regularly dated Vicki Hodge and often stayed weekends at her flat opposite Bishop's Park. But that didn't stop him having sex with another society beauty at her apartment in South Kensington. One day the woman's flatmate, Shaun Redmayne, answered the front door to Vicky. 'She burst into my flatmate's bedroom and found Bindon in bed with this woman. He came flying out of the room fast. He thought I was some criminal who'd come with Vicki to the flat and knocked me to the floor. I stayed down and Bindon dashed out the front door. Meanwhile, Vicki and my flatmate were scratching each other's eyes out. It was bedlam.'

The following day, Redmayne bumped into Bindon in a local pub and Bindon apologised profusely for hitting him. 'I thought you was some geezer she'd brought along to have a dig at me,' explained Bindon.

Not long afterwards, Bindon got himself a part in a play called *Cater Street* at the world-famous Old Vic, starring Vanessa Redgrave and Robert Shaw. But that didn't stop him going on a mammoth drinking session with Shaun Redmayne, who later explained, 'It was an outrageous afternoon of boozing, especially when you consider Bindon had to be at the Old Vic by seven-thirty that evening. Then we all came back to the flat and he started bonking my flatmate. They were having sex over and over. I was shouting at the door because I knew he was going to miss the play. Then he finally got a cab at seven-thirty and got there to find the cast and crew all outside the theatre after a bomb threat had been rung in.' Redmayne is convinced Bindon rang in the threat because he knew he wasn't in a fit state to tread the boards that evening.

Vicki was so furious about Bindon's latest indiscretion with Redmayne's flatmate that she told him she wanted a complete break in their relationship. But it didn't last long. Less than two months later they had a reunion at a friend's country cottage. 'I was feeling confident,' she later remembered. 'I knew I was suntanned and desirable, and we sat on the four-poster bed looking at each other. I said, "Well, have you missed me?" And he replied, "Of course I've bloody missed you." I leaned over and kissed him – and that was the end of the talking. We just clambered into the four-poster and made love. I don't think we slept at all that night. For me, the good times were here again. I forgot all about the bad things between us.'

Vicki and Bindon spent a fortnight together in the country and then returned to London with him pledging to set up home with her in Fulham. He appeared to have changed his ways, and her happiness was apparently complete.

Chapter Six

Bindon's Saturday rugby games eventually petered out, to be replaced with Frisbee-throwing sessions in a couple of parks close to his family's home in Peterborough Road. He was introduced to Frisbee by his old friend, eccentric New York actor Benny Carruthers. One Saturday he showed up for a game with his friend to find Hollywood actor Elliot Gould – who unknown to Bindon had already had a brief fling with Vicki – and another American actor called Greg Hodal. 'Benny introduced me to this friend of his,' Hodal later recalled, 'who was built like a brick shithouse and seemed to be a very tough guy. He started rabbitting and was right in my face and I thought, Man, this is going to be quite a game. I thought I was going to have to fight this guy. I wondered what would happen and whether I would get out of there alive.'

That man, of course, was John Bindon and this

relationship, just like so many of his closest friendships, was to start on a virtual war footing. It was as if Bindon had to test the hardness of other men before deciding if he could trust them. That evening, he introduced Greg Hodal to Vicki. 'This Little Bo Peep kinda girl in a mini-skirt turns up and it's Vicki Hodge. Then this act started where he spun her around and it was just part of their routine. I thought, Oh, man, what a dude! It was only then I realised they were lovers.' Bindon, Vicki and Greg went to dinner that evening at Mr Chow's in Earls Court Road, and a close friendship was hatched.

But Greg knew only too well that he could so easily have failed Bindon's test when they first met. 'With John it was down to the way you handled yourself. He was looking to see if I had real pride and didn't bottle out to him. I'd sometimes met other people who'd say they were going to get John and asked me what I thought about that. I'd say I didn't think it was a good idea. He was my mate and I wanted to show him 100 per cent loyalty. You don't just sit there and say it's fine. And believe me, there were some very heavy-duty guys asking around town about John Bindon.'

Some rival villains tried to suggest that Bindon's high-profile existence was a deliberate ploy because he was a secret police informant. Greg slammed such gossip. 'Bindon hated the Old Bill. He used to say, "The only honest policemen you'll ever see is possibly the man right at the top and the ones who get kids across zebra crossings. All the other ones with their moody blue raincoats and tough boots, they're all bent."' It was virtually word for word what he'd said in his role as a wife-beating husband

Chapter Six

in *Poor Cow*. Now Bindon was using his dramatic roles to improve his criminal kudos.

Greg Hodal was more than just another passing show-business friend. He knew a lot of the actors who had just started work on a film called *Barry Lyndon* with Ryan O'Neal and Marisa Berenson and directed by the legendary Stanley Kubrick. This adaptation of William Makepeace Thackeray's classic novel must have seemed very foreign to Bindon, but he became obsessed with getting a role in the film after hearing about it.

'Kubrick offered me a part one night in Ireland where they were filming,' Greg explained, 'because one of his actors had failed a screen test. I was flattered but couldn't do the part because I was working on another movie in Ireland. But I told Kubrick I had a friend who'd be brilliant for the role. I immediately called John in London and said, "Listen, if you want a part in Stanley's film I can get it for you." They got him a plane ticket and he flew over for a test.'

Bindon met up with Greg before his audition in Waterford in the south of Eire where the film was located. 'I took John out into the woods so we could rehearse his lines. It was a recruitment speech because he was to play a recruiter in the movie and he was trying to get men to join the English army. It was quite a long speech and he had to stand on a stump in the town square to deliver it. John and I rehearsed it over and over again until he had it word perfect. We even tape-recorded it and played it at dinner just to make sure it was right.'

Next morning, Bindon was so nervous on his way to the set to be auditioned by Kubrick that he got his driver to stop the car so he could vomit on the side of the road. But all went well. 'John delivered the speech perfectly and did it a couple of times for different cameras and Stanley came over and said it was great. He was extremely happy.' The part only lasted a day, but for Bindon it was a wonderful morale-booster at a time when his acting work seemed to be drying up.

A few months later, Greg rang Bindon from his home in California and asked if he could rent a room in his tiny house in Chesham Mews. Greg was stunned at just how small it was when he turned up there a few days later. 'It had a front room with a fireplace, but it was maybe seven feet across. The bedroom had no windows, a couple of tortoiseshell lamps, and there was a tiny kitchen with a table in it and a Metropolitan Police clock nicked out of a police station. The front room became my bedroom and I stayed for about seven months.'

Many of Greg's friends in London predicted that living with Bindon would end in disaster. 'A few people actually said to me, "He'll kill you." But they didn't know John very well.' As Greg gained Bindon's complete and utter trust, he started to take the young American actor to some unusual west-London haunts. 'We'd usually go out for a pub lunch at The Roebuck on the King's Road and then, when the pub closed, we'd go to a private drinking club. There was one on the King's Road up near the fire station. We'd also pop in to Terry de Havilland's shoe shop opposite The Roebuck. He had this cellar under the shop where we'd have a little spliff or whatever. Pot was a calming thing for John. He needed it to relax and it made him a much safer guy to be around.'

When Greg suggested that he and Bindon take a trip

Chapter Six

south of the river to a pub that had been recommended to him, Bindon gently explained to his new young friend that going into south London might prove a bit of problem. 'There's a few fellas there who might take a pop at me, Greg,' he said, ever so casually. Greg never again suggested a trip south of the river. However, they did venture to the Elephant and Castle in order to visit Bindon's former lover Sheila and daughter Kelly. 'Sheila seemed very uptight whenever I met her with John because she didn't like the way John had dumped her for his new rich, show-business friends – including Vicki, of course. I kept a low profile, but it was obviously important to John to keep in touch with his daughter, so he put up with a bit of mouth from Sheila.'

Back in west London, Bindon seemed increasingly more at home with Greg and other actors who now included Ryan O'Neal back from filming *Barry Lyndon* in Ireland. Weekend Frisbee sessions had become a regular occurrence and, afterwards, Bindon and some of his famous new friends often visited Vicki Hodge's flat where he would cook for them all. During these lunches, Greg found himself intrigued by Bindon's knowledge. 'John was incredibly well read and was always trying to better himself. We played a lot of Scrabble together, which John was very good at.'

One day, Bindon and Greg were over at the nearby home of Bindon's agent and friend Tony Howard playing Scrabble while Howard's wife Nancy cooked them all Sunday lunch. 'Tony was playing,' Greg remembers, 'plus a guy who did lights for Pink Floyd. But then Tony took forty-five minutes for his turn. John got a bit pissed off. "You gotta move faster, Tone," he told him. Finally,

Howard put down the word CAT for five points. All that time for CAT – it was ridiculous. No double letter. Nothing. Unbelievable. Bindon went loopy and demanded that we changed the rules right there and then and agreed to a one-minute time rule. For the following few weeks, me and John swatted up on the dictionary back at Chesham Mews. Many nights we played four or five games over a period of three hours or more. It was fast and it never got boring. John was highly competitive and didn't like losing, but we never had any trouble between us. We were two very different guys and we never once came to blows.'

Bindon told Greg he adored working with stars. 'Just imagine me,' he said proudly, 'a tearaway kid from the slums, hobnobbing with famous people like Richard Harris and Mick Jagger.' He made a point of studying the way these famous actors moved and held themselves: they were real, professional performers and he constantly tried to learn from them.

Back home in Fulham, Bindon was also enjoying his own small measure of fame, although life inside the family remained unchanged. But his inner confidence was now even more immense thanks to the challenge of acting. And then there were the women – Bindon had them gathering around him like bees to a honeypot. He was a prize to them. Girls would always be his downfall – he just revelled in the idea of being loved by them all, and flirted outrageously with virtually every woman he met. And he liked to make sure Vicki Hodge heard about most of his conquests.

Terry de Havilland had attached himself to the hard man knowing full well he was a veritable babe magnet.

Chapter Six

'Bindon and I used to seriously go out on the pull. Two or three chicks a day. We'd pull 'em outside The Roebuck or anywhere else we could lay our hands on them, and they loved it,' he recalled.

And John's capacity for practical jokes continued. One day he and de Havilland were in an expensive restaurant in Fulham Road when Bindon decided to complain about the spaghetti. As the waiter approached, he opened his mouth and spat out a live maggot. 'We got a refund and left the place in stitches. Bindon had got the maggots from his brother who was into fishing.'

On another occasion, de Havilland and Bindon were in a Chelsea villains' haunt called J Arthur's when Bindon spotted a man he didn't like. 'They apparently had some history, and John was well pissed off that this character was drinking on his manor. Bindon popped in the loo then came out and slipped some mercury in this other fella's drink. Seconds later he's rushing to the toilet but he can't get off the seat because John had superglued it. The fire brigade had to be called and there's this so-called hard man sitting there in front of everyone and he can't even get his trousers up. They had to cut out the seat and walk him through the club to the ambulance. How humiliating is that?'

But there was a serious side to all this practical joking. Bindon was clearly hated by certain other criminals, and began regularly carrying a knife down the side of his python-skin cowboy boots which were part of his own special 'uniform' that also included blue jeans and a T-shirt. Terry de Havilland says he never questioned where Bindon received his income at this time. 'I never saw John in gainful employment. He was a good actor, but he didn't get that much work.' Nevertheless, he loved chatting about his career as an actor, and had a seemingly permanent audience in the pubs and clubs of Chelsea and Fulham. Back at Chesham Mews, he adored getting out his photo albums to talk visitors through his life. 'He'd talk about how he'd appeared at the Old Vic and how they used to fill out his pants with tissue to make him look like he had an even bigger dick than he already had for all the poofs in the front row during the matinees,' de Havilland recalled. 'John had a story for everything.'

When Bindon strayed away from Fulham and Chelsea, he ended up in bother. One time he was drinking in a pub in Portobello Road when another drinker picked a fight with him. Bindon demolished the man in seconds, but someone called the police and he soon found himself sitting in the back of a squad car about to be nicked for GBH. The arresting officer said he was willing to forget the whole incident if Bindon went and bashed up this big guy who drank in the same pub. Bindon was up for it and returned later that night. The intended target was quietly sipping a pint near the bar when he barged in. Terry de Havilland only knows about the story because Bindon took him back to the pub the following night to show him the man's blood splatter on the ceiling, which Bindon called 'a right result'. He said he had punched the guy so hard he had virtually exploded.

Back on his manor, anyone stupid enough to take on Bindon paid the price. De Havilland witnessed an attack by Bindon on a huge Irishman in The Water Rat after the other man 'took exception to Bindon pulling his cock out'.

Chapter Six

'John told this other fella to shut it, but this guy kept coming towards him. Bindon had to be careful that night because he'd broken all his knuckles down the years and there was only one that was in good working order that evening. But all of a sudden he leaped virtually over my shoulder and caught this other guy with a massive right and he was knocked out cold. Just one punch did it. Down like a sack of potatoes.'

Bindon particularly detested the drug dealers who hung around certain pubs like bloodsuckers trying to sell hard narcotics such as cocaine and heroin. 'One young dealer called Belfast was kicked all the way up the King's Road when he tried to flog some gear under Bindon's nose,' said de Havilland. Later that same evening Bindon and a couple of pals smashed up another dealer's den just off Fulham Road as a warning to them to stay away from the pubs he went in. 'John might have liked – and needed – a puff of weed now and again to calm his nerves, but he wouldn't tolerate anyone trying to flog the heavy stuff in his presence,' explained one old pal.

Bindon's friends and enemies presumed he was coining it in as a famous actor, but in reality many of his TV and film roles were not highly paid, so he was obliged to earn an additional crust when and where he could find it. Many of the landlords of the pubs he frequented felt indebted to Bindon for keeping scumbag drug dealers out of their premises, so some of them even bunged him payments now and again for keeping their premises 'clean'. One of his oldest friends explained, 'Originally John was seeing off these characters because he felt it was his duty. He wasn't after paying, but some landlords realised it made sense to keep him sweet and it kept all the vermin away.' Unfortunately, he sometimes went a little too far in his efforts to 'protect' the law-abiding customers in his most regular haunts. One night he accidentally laid into a pub manager, leaving him with a broken jaw after what was later described as 'a little misunderstanding'. 'I've never been hit so hard in my life,' the man recalled a few years later.

It was certainly true that an even heavier element of unpredictability was creeping into John Bindon's behaviour, and that was proving frightening to people who didn't want to end up on the receiving end of one of his fists. It wasn't helped by his continuing habit of pulling out his 'old chap' whenever he felt like shocking the customers. His old pal Roy Dennis recalled, 'One time he put his prick on the hotplate in the Chelsea Potter and the landlady chased him out with a brush. John was always good for a laugh, but there were times when he pushed his luck.'

Bindon also occasionally earned a few extra bob as a runner for a King's Road antique dealer, and it was through him that he met an attractive brunette jazz and blues singer called Dana Gillespie. Dana had been born a baroness and spent a traditional silver-spoon childhood among the English upper classes in a world of nannies and servants. Her playmates came from Eton and Harrow. But somewhere along the way things changed so drastically that her priorities became music and men. Her first serious love affair was with David Bowie; Bob Dylan, Jimmy Page, Keith Moon and P. J. Proby followed. She even once admitted bedding Angie and David Bowie at the same time. Dana's flat was only a ten-minute walk from

Chapter Six

Bindon's little house in Chesham Mews; he was soon a regular visitor en route to all his other favoured haunts. 'I was always at home in the afternoons because, being a singer, I worked at night,' Dana later explained. 'He had a lot of friends he'd pass his time with and loved dropping in here. When I was in rehearsals in the West End, I'd sometimes leap in a limo, go and have a drink with Biffo and then go back to rehearsals afterwards. He was extremely entertaining company.'

At one stage Dana Gillespie was working on a record at Island Studios just off Portobello Road. 'Bindon would come in every day like a resident court jester. He loved being with musicians. One time we even secretly recorded him telling stories while he was in the studio and spent months playing him back the most embarrassing parts.' Dana also took dozens and dozens of Polaroid photos of Bindon with her friends that she still treasures to this day. 'They were good times and John was the most important part of it all back then.'

Dana has always insisted she and Bindon were 'like brother and sister', but there was a dark side to their relationship. 'Vicki would often hang about outside my home when she thought Bindon was in here with me. I remember one time he looked out of the window and said she had been outside for hours in a taxi following him and checking him out. He'd say, "Oh, she's still there," or whatever. I always felt bad about that because I knew she presumed I was sleeping with Bindon, which I really wasn't. In the end, she got to know the truth and realised I was no threat to her.'

After the air had been cleared, Vicki accompanied

Bindon and Dana to a huge party given by Victor Lownes, the boss of the London Playboy Club, at his country pile, Stocks in Hertfordshire. Vicki turned up wearing little more than a T-shirt; but Bindon's attention was caught by two other beautiful women at the party – Lownes's attractive publicity assistant Serena Williams and David Bowie's zany wife Angie. Nothing happened at the actual party, but both women made a play for Bindon and he was like a kid in a candy shop. Vicki was ignored as he spent the whole night flirting with the two women.

So it was no surprise when Bindon and Vicki were invited to visit the house Angie Bowie shared with David in Oakley Street, Chelsea. Vicki later explained that, 'Angie had a beautiful house that was always filled with people twenty-four hours a day. It was a non-stop party.' A few days after that first visit, Bindon disappeared and Vicki turned up at the house and waited outside for him – she may have suspected he was in bed with Angie Bowie and/or some of her famous friends. At one stage she got so impatient with waiting that she started hurling milk bottles at the windows to try and get his attention. Afterwards they had a furious row and she warned him to stay away from Angie.

Back in the seventies, there were no limits as far as Angie Bowie and her friends were concerned. Terry de Havilland says it was well known that Bindon was one of her favourites, mainly because of the size of his penis. 'She once got five of her friends to screw Bindon all at the same time and then watched the whole thing. It was outrageous. Lucky fella!' says de Havilland.

Bindon himself spoke many years later about his

Chapter Six

encounters with Angie. 'One old lover fixed up my affair with David Bowie's ex-wife Angie. She told her about my "talent". Angie was Lakes of Killarney [barmy]. I got to her house once to find five really knockout girls lined up in the scantiest of black underwear, stockings and high heels. They all said, "Hello, Johnny," and piled into me. What can I say, I gave them my best shot! I couldn't believe I got to do the business with these amazing and willing ladies. It was the sort of fantasy situation it would cost a fortune to set up.'

One of Bindon's oldest friends says that all five of the women Bindon slept with that day were the wives of other rock stars. 'Bindon would never say exactly who they were because he was quite a gentleman in that way, but he said he was a bunged a few bob afterwards when he found out that the husbands of these women had encouraged them to sleep with him.'

And another source who had known Angie Bowie for many years insisted that Bindon was paid on a number of occasions to sleep with some of her women friends. 'Bindon didn't seem to mind about it and he became like the hired stud who would keep them satisfied. A couple of the husbands even watched him having sex with their wives,' recalled the source.

One source says that Bindon was allowed by David Bowie to make love to his wife while Mick Jagger was nearby. 'He was proud of his performances at Bowie's house. He said it was kind of freaky to have two of the most famous rock stars in the world in the same house while he screwed Angie. John said that, after he'd satisfied her, he left the three of them in the house together. It was bizarre.'

Another of Bindon's former lovers told this author that on at least one occasion Mick Jagger, David Bowie and John Bindon were all lovers of Angie Bowie at the same time. 'John said there were burn marks on the sheets, and so did Angie! I was having a fling with John at the same time and there was a black girl called Shelagh who was Angie's lover. It might sound shocking to some people, but this sort of thing was happening all the time back then. Angie and Vicki Hodge were pretty blunt. They'd walk into a club, grab a man and say things like, "How are you? Do you want me?" It was shocking to me. It's very assertive, and to tell you the truth I don't think John really liked girls doing that, but he was a bit scared of both Vicki and Angie and he couldn't help being impressed by the famous names who were always round at the Bowie house.'

Dana Gillespie summed it all up when she said many years later, 'Bindon's affair with Angie was purely about sex, not love.'

At the Bowie's 1973 Christmas party, Bindon was encouraged to walk around with a big red dildo strapped to his forehead. Angie later admitted that she had encouraged him to do so and intended to seduce him that same night. Paul and Linda McCartney were also at the party and started singing carols – one person who attended the party said that Bindon sang along heartily, complete with red dildo.

Angie Bowie and others even dreamed up a new name for Bindon's twelve-inch penis. 'They called it "The Mighty Marrow" because it was long and fat,' explained one of his former lovers.

Chapter Six

Angie has never denied her sexual involvement with a host of people, including Bindon. In her book about her marriage to David Bowie, she regularly referred to Bindon and his big organ. She also constantly referred to drug and sex orgies at the house in Oakley Street. As she later explained, 'Free love was natural and simply what one did. The pill was the great catalyst and liberator. Sex has always been a serious interest of mine and I had no intention of getting monogamously involved with someone who'd already said they weren't in love with me.'

Shortly after this, Bindon's world was significantly widened when he agreed to work as a so-called 'strong-arm man' with Dana Gillespie who was accompanying David Bowie on his tour of the states. America was a hell of an eye-opener to Bindon, who had rarely been out of the UK before. However, as Dana later disclosed, Bindon did sometimes take his duties a little bit too seriously. 'One time in New York I was doing a special gala night with Bowie, Bette Midler and Janet Leigh and I told Bindon I didn't want to see anyone before the show started as I was a little nervous. Unknown to me, an old tramp came up to him outside a few minutes later and said he wanted to see me and told Bindon to tell me that "Bob's here". But Bindon replied, "I don't care if you're Bob Dylan. You can fuck off." That's precisely who it was! Later on, I went down for a sound check and found Dylan queuing up dressed as the old tramp. He said he'd been afraid to challenge Bindon in case he got a right-hander!'

Bindon loved being on a rock 'n' roll tour. As Dana explained, 'We visited a place called the Bijou Theatre in Philadelphia and stayed at the Barclay Hotel, and that night Bindon was supposed to pick up all the gate money and look after me as well, but instead he pulled some bird who turned out to be a complete nutter and ended up giving her one all night long. It was very embarrassing because all his shouts and cries could be heard by the rest of us staying on the same floor as him. But, worse than that, when he woke up the next morning all the gate money was missing. It was tens of thousands of dollars so we were not best pleased with Mr Bindon.

'The trouble with Bindon was that he was in his element on tour. I was probably stupid to get him involved in the first place. But then Bindon was always led by his dick. There were a lot of laughs out on the road, but we had to more of less babysit him because he just couldn't stay out of trouble.'

On Bindon's return to Fulham, he and Vicki started virtually living together, but by now they had entered an altogether darker and more terrifying stage in their relationship. Gangsters were regularly hiring him to beat up their enemies, and his frustration with the acting profession did nothing to calm his violent rages. Sometimes he would literally break down the door to their flat in a fury. Another time he ripped off the door of Vicki's car and accidentally almost snapped the tops of three of her fingers off. Bindon was devastated that he'd allowed his moodiness to take such control of their lives. After one of these terrifying rages, the couple would have yet another heart to heart before retiring to the bedroom to make love all night long. It seemed to be the only way they could calm themselves.

One night, Bindon received a late phone call from a

Chapter Six

criminal associate saying he needed some help with a man who was refusing to pay off a long-standing debt. Bindon grabbed his sheaf knife, which he always kept nearby at night, and rang for a minicab to take him to a house in Shepherds Bush. Three hours later, he slipped back into bed alongside Vicki. He was shaking violently and refused to say what had happened.

Bindon's violence escalated as the acting work dried up. He was addicted to stardom but unable to get any really big roles to satisfy his lust for fame. It was a catch-22 situation: he was losing acting jobs because of his uncontrollable behaviour. And becoming buddies with one of the most notoriously hard-living people in show business didn't exactly help calm John Bindon down. Richard Cole, legendary road manager for Led Zeppelin and other big rock 'n' roll acts, was introduced to Bindon by the group's larger-than-life manager Peter Grant. 'Peter wanted me to help Bindon sort out a bit of bother he had with someone who was threatening to go to the police after a fight,' explained Cole. 'I knew this fella so I was able to calm the situation down and avoid any aggro. In any case, I liked Bindon. I felt relaxed in his company and we became close mates very quickly.'

At the time Cole had just finished working with Eric Clapton on his *461 Ocean Boulevard* tour and he was spending a lot time at the Zeppelin offices on the King's Road. He was also a regular at Bindon's favourite haunts The Water Rat, The Roebuck and The Man in The Moon. 'Sometimes I ended up staying the night at Vicki's flat because I was too pissed to drive home to the country,' explained Cole. He noticed that the flat was 'like something out of a bygone era. It was stuffed with all this old-fashioned furniture she must have got from her wedding to Ian Heath. It all looked a bit dated to me. On Saturday afternoons I got into the habit of having a puff and watching the rugby. Bindon would do the cooking and it was a pretty relaxed atmosphere.'

More and more, Bindon found himself being challenged to fights in pubs across the manor. He usually flattened all-comers in seconds, but, when one character called Kenny objected to the way he was talking to his girlfriend in The Water Rat and the two men stepped outside, he found himself on the receiving end of something he wasn't expecting. 'Kenny had a right set-to with Bindon and gave him a good hiding,' a witness to the fight later explained. 'I think it's the only time I ever saw Bindon beaten.' It was a bad omen: Bindon had always prided himself on being king of his manor, and that beating seemed to suggest he might be losing his touch. There were too many diversions around, and Bindon had stopped constantly watching his back as most faces did in Fulham. He seemed vulnerable for the first time in years.

Not long after this, he clashed with a couple of South African rugby players at his local, The Star. A witness to the fight explained what happened: 'Bindon was right cocky and said, "I'm going to have those two," after getting annoyed at a few comments they were making. So he starts a row over what's the strongest beer. Then he hits out at one guy and picks the other one up by the crotch and the neck, turns him over and hits his head down on the floor over and over again. Those fellas never came back to The Star in a hurry.' That fight convinced Bindon he was

CHAPTER SIX

still on top of his game; but his feelings of rejection as an actor persisted. He had so desperately wanted to turn his back on criminality for good, but now he was immersing himself in villainy once more because there seemed no other way to stay afloat financially.

And old habits died very hard for John Bindon. Strolling into The Britannia one day, he noticed that Fred Hayes, the son of owners George and Nora, was involved in a vicious fight outside. It was Fred's twentieth birthday. He takes up the story: 'I'd knocked this fella flat out and was dragging him round to an alleyway when Bindon turned up and told me to leave the bloke to him because it was my birthday and I should go in and enjoy myself. So that's what I did. Trouble was, these other geezers saw Bindon dragging their brother into the alley and presumed it was Bindon who'd hurt him. Next day they laid into Bindon in another boozer.' It seemed that even when John Bindon thought he was doing someone a favour it landed him in hot water. No longer did everything he touch turn to gold.

But at least he hadn't yet lost his ability to seduce a pretty girl. A stunning Swedish model called Mona had just finished an unhappy marriage to a fashion designer when she met Bindon in the Chelsea Hot Pot restaurant in the King's Road. She had no idea who either he or Vicki Hodge were at the time, but she later told friends that Bindon was very easy to talk to and that they 'got on like a house on fire'. Later that night Bindon took Mona back to the house in Chesham Mews. She was impressed by the address, but that was before she walked into the property: Mona later described the house as 'weird'. 'He had a picture of the devil as a black man with a huge willy screwing a white girl in an oil painting above his bed. It was a bit scary. I suppose you could call it intriguing because you walked in and went straight up the stairs because of a garage alongside it. There was no central heating and it was freezing. The biggest room was the bedroom, which was lucky because we managed to keep warm in there. Upstairs was the tiny kitchen and a small loo plus a den with a few pillows scattered across the floor.' The arch-seducer didn't even provide any music or booze for his new conquest. 'We just went straight to the bedroom, but he was very polite. We did it all night, although I have to say he was not a great love-maker. He couldn't kiss properly because he seemed out of breath. After a while I made it my job to teach him how to kiss. After a few nights together I told him that he was absolutely useless, because he didn't know where the bits and bobs were. He thought this was hilarious and later told everyone we knew what I'd said. At least he could laugh at himself. Most men would be devastated, but he didn't mind me saying it. I think John thought he was a good enough lover just because of his big willy. He didn't seem to bother with anything else. That was enough in his mind.'

To some girls, including Mona, Bindon had virtually the same mentality as a hooker. Kissing didn't seem important to him. He also used to get incredibly shy when Mona tried to get emotional with him. 'He'd giggle and get embarrassed and try to avoid the issue. He was a walking contradiction.' But perhaps the biggest revelation from Mona was about Bindon's 'weapon'. 'It was just as big as they said, and he wasn't circumcised, but he was gentle with it. However, John was so proud of it that it sometimes

Chapter Six

drove me nuts because he'd go on about it so much. Sometimes he freaked people out in the pub by flashing it. Girls I knew were obsessed with how big it got when it was hard because it seemed so big when it was soft. But, in fact, it wasn't much bigger hard. I've seen it both ways and I can assure you it's not that different!'

Bindon's affair with Mona eventually fizzled out. Shortly afterwards, she encountered Vicki Hodge in bizarre circumstances in The Water Rat. 'Everyone had told me how formidable Vicki could be, and there I was sitting on the toilet when she knocks on my cubicle, bold as brass. I thought, Oh my God, what's she going to do to me? When I walked out I was a little scared, but she just said, "What are you doing with him when you can have a choice of anybody?" Then she put her arms around me, which was very suspicious. But I didn't let on that I'd had the affair with John in case she was trying to trick me. Then Vicki looked right close up to me and said ever so sweetly, "Nice girls don't sleep with other girls' men." John and Vicki deserved each other in many ways. He was always puffing himself up as a tough guy, and she seemed to get off on that.'

A few months later, Vicki bizarrely asked Mona if she would move into her flat and look after her dogs while she was abroad. 'Everywhere you sat in that flat you sat on one of her bloody Yorkshire terriers. God knows how John put up with it, but the strangest thing was that she was prepared to have me look after her home even though she suspected I'd slept with her boyfriend.' Mona briefly rekindled her affair with Bindon while staying at Vicki's flat, but it soon faded out again. She encountered him many times over the following twenty years. 'I think Vicki and John had a very strange relationship,' she recalled. 'She was terribly, terribly jealous, but she was also a very naughty girl. I didn't have much time for her and she didn't for me. She just talks the way the newspapers want to hear. I never actually fell in love with John but I think he liked me because I was his first foreign girlfriend. I was quite well spoken. I was his little pretty Swede. John knew he was never a true provider and in that way he was very aware of his own faults. He really did know that he could not bring home the bacon. But there was something about his personality. Being around him was so much fun and if he liked you he was so protective.'

Meanwhile, other adventures were beckoning for John Bindon.

Chapter Seven

John Bindon was delighted when he was offered the chance of a holiday of a lifetime by his new singer friend Dana Gillespie. He undoubtedly needed a break from his domestic problems, lack of acting work and increasingly frequent run-ins with other criminals, although at first, when she invited him to join her on the deserted private Caribbean island of Mustique, he thought she was just winding him up. Or in his own words, 'Dana was one hell of a practical joker and I thought she was pulling my plonker until I realised she meant it.'

Bindon caught a plane to Barbados not even realising that he would then have to get to Mustique by boat. 'I thought it was just a flight connection – I didn't know it was almost inaccessible. In the end I conned my way there on this flaming great yacht. The first geezer I saw when I waded on to the beach was this hulking black man. I said,

"Do you know Dana Gillespie?"

'"Yeah! Are you Biffo the Bear?"

'I discovered he was Basil Charles, who ran the beach bar and lived with a titled girl. He took me on his bike to where Dana was staying with her mate, composer Lionel Bart. It was a great-looking house and the island was the sort of tropical paradise I'd only seen in the Bounty ads on telly. There weren't a lot of people around – it ain't Southend. And the ones you do see are a select band of filthy-rich who have villas there, like Princess Margaret and Colin Tennant – he's the man who decides if you get an intro to "PM", as her lot call her. He makes sure she doesn't mix with any toerags. After all, he did own the island. He gave me some tips on what to do, like, "Don't talk to her until she talks to you."

'So I amble up to The Cotton House, which is the most amazing flash gaff where PM gives lunch and dinner parties for all the nobs. Dana introduces me and we just sort of said hello. I remember thinking what nice skin she had. The gaff was designed by a mate of Noel Coward's, and was like some bleedin' great palace out of the British Raj. We all sat down to dinner and it was like the last great bastion of the Empire. Everyone was in evening dress and dickie bows. It was all white tablecloths, black waiters and loads of silver to puzzle you – which knife and fork to use.

'She seemed very much her own girl, not daft at all. But my accent and my cockney phrases foxed her sometimes. We talked about PG Wodehouse, acting, films and showbiz. Sometimes she'd laugh and I had to explain what I was saying, like, "Gay and Hearty or Moriaty means party, Ma'am," and "Apples and pears is stairs."

Chapter Seven

'She asked me, "What's a wally? Is it the same as a toby, that word you used earlier?" When I said yes, she said, "How silly, two words for the same thing."'

Bindon was soon in his element. 'Shortly after he arrived a couple of girls I knew turned up and one of them took a fancy to Bindon,' recalled Dana. 'Everyone on the island sunbathed nude, so Bindon's penis was soon a very big talking point with everyone and he enjoyed a bit of fun with one of the girls.' Eventually, he ended up making love to the woman just a few feet away from where Dana was doing her beadwork, under the shade of a nearby eucalyptus tree. Meanwhile, Lionel Bart was nearby in bed, nursing a terrible hangover. Dana continued, 'Well, just behind the bush where Bindon was having it off with this long-legged white girl was a group of local teenage lads having a wank while watching them. And there behind the net curtains was gay Lionel in his room having a wank over the boys. It was a hilarious chain reaction that we all laughed about for days afterwards.'

With no electricity and just candles for light, there was little to do before sunrise or after sunset. But Dana explained that Bindon coped admirably. 'He was fabulous company. He'd got away from all the pressures in London and was enjoying doing little or nothing. I have an image of him frozen in time, standing on a rock in the ocean posing for us and then looking out to sea like some forlorn sea captain. He said the trip was the happiest time of his life and I'm sure he meant it. He had never been in such a peaceful environment. I think that trip helped change him as a character.'

Bindon saw quite a lot of Princess Margaret during those

three weeks on the island. 'Her beach parties weren't exactly a snack on the sands,' he recalled. 'A fleet of cars would set all the guests down, plus the maids, tables, crockery, silver and glass. PM would be in a strapless costume or loose kaftan with her cigarette in one hand and a drink in the other.'

Mustique was unique because the company on the island was drawn from all classes and backgrounds. Colin Tennant had even been responsible for introducing PM to her controversial young friend Roddy Llewellyn in the early seventies. The relaxed mood on Mustique was epitomised one day when Tennant was on the beach with Margaret and Roddy. Another man, Nicholas Courtney, asked her, 'Would you mind, Ma'am, if I took off my trunks?' She did not object and the others undressed too. The princess then took pictures of them all.

Bindon was so short of clothes at one stage when he was on Mustique that he borrowed a T-shirt from Dana emblazoned with the words 'Enjoy Cocaine', written in the same style as the Coca-Cola logo. 'And that's how pictures were taken of me sitting next to PM wearing my "Enjoy Cocaine" T-shirt. I think she liked me 'cos I nattered away quite happily and you couldn't impose on her if she didn't want to know. PM let her hair down more at some of the night-time parties where Colin would lay on a bit of entertainment. Like the night we all sang saucy calypsos.'

But there was a clearly defined etiquette when it came to dealing with Princess Margaret, even on the laid-back island of Mustique. Dana Gillespie explained, 'I asked her what I should call her and she said, "Ma'am, just like a Christian name." You never went to her house. But we all

Chapter Seven

happened to be on the same beach one day when Colin Tennant was cooking up a couple of lobsters. PM was very easy-going and she went for a swim and a lot of the people there didn't even know who she was at first. At one point I remember John was talking to her and telling her funny stories – although very respectfully calling her Ma'am. Then he started singing, "Marks & Spencer's, she gets her knickers at Marks & Spencer's!" It was hilarious, and John had broken the ice brilliantly, as usual.'

Bindon and Margaret laughed and joked for hours on end, holding sing-songs round a piano, and also attended outdoor parties on the island's deserted beaches. After Dana left the island, Bindon started to run out of money, but he ended up scraping through for a few more weeks by staying with Basil Charles. He also saw Princess Margaret on at least three more occasions, and later admitted to one friend that something happened between them on one of the beaches – although he never expanded on precisely what.

Dana Gillespie explained, 'There were other meetings, but I wasn't there. Princess Margaret pretty much lived in a world of her own, but Bindon was discreet. He would never have told if something did happen between them …' She is reluctant to talk in any more detail about Bindon's first trip to Mustique. When she opened her photo album to show some pictures, the famous cocaine T-shirt photo was missing. 'Vicki turned up at my home one day years later and asked to borrow it, and I never saw it again,' she explained.

However, one of Bindon's other lovers during his first trip to the Caribbean broke a thirty-year silence to tell this author from her home in Spain about what really happened between Bindon and Princess Margaret. 'John was mighty proud of the size of his willy, but he was even more proud of what happened between him and the princess. He swore me to secrecy, but admitted that he'd slept with her on Mustique just a couple of days before we met. I don't know why he only told me. I guess he thought that because I was a local girl I'd never end up telling anyone important. I wasn't that interested in what he was saying at the time because I thought it was no big deal. Everyone has a more relaxed attitude towards sex out there. That's why I liked Bindon. He was more like a West Indian than a white boy. He loved to make love. It was like the fuel that kept him going and he was great to be with.'

Bindon was certainly enough of a hit with 'PM' to be asked to come back to the island the following year for a longer stay, and he pledged to bring Vicki with him this time.

Back in London, Bindon became a regular at a club in Chelsea called the Gasworks, a bizarre establishment favoured by a combination of aristocrats and criminals. Princess Margaret also became a regular visitor to the club at this time. One of Bindon's friends remembered, 'John saw a lot of Margaret after that first trip to Mustique, and he said that she sometimes sent a car round to pick him up and bring him to her at Kensington Palace. But he wouldn't say any more than that.'

Another one of Bindon's oldest friends said, 'I remember seeing John sitting chatting in a very relaxed manner with Princess Margaret in the Gasworks. She was surrounded by people, including Roddy Llewellyn, but she only had

Chapter Seven

eyes for John. She seemed to be eating out of his hand. I knew then that something was going on between them.'

Yet another friend told this author that Bindon let slip to him that PM regularly sent a car round to pick him up and bring him for love trysts at her royal apartments in Kensington Palace. 'John had a relationship with Margaret and it flourished for a short while after he got back from Mustique, but he was very nervous about mentioning it,' said the source. 'I only know about it because one time I was at the mews house when he got a call from one of her people to say that a car was coming round to pick him up. I pressed him on what was going on and he blurted it out, but then got me to swear not to mention it to anyone. This is the first time I've told anyone.'

It's not clear precisely how many times Bindon visited Margaret at Kensington Palace but, according to other sources, 'something was going on for at least a few months' after his return from that first trip to Mustique.

The following December, Bindon and Vicki Hodge found themselves having lunch on Mustique's Macaroni Beach with Princess Margaret. Also present were Colin Tennant, Dana Gillespie and her friend Leslie Spitz. Vicki later described the trip to Mustique as 'the best holiday I've had in my life'. She and Bindon had already enjoyed a fortnight of making love and relaxing before Princess Margaret arrived on the island. They even joined a reception party to greet Margaret's plane. Bindon was welcomed so warmly by the princess that Vicki later told a friend, 'I felt a pang of jealousy. I thought, She may be a princess, but he's my man.'

Over the next few days Vicki got used to watching her

lover lavish attention on Margaret. At parties he lit her cigarettes and made sure her glass was filled with chilled champagne, and at luxurious beachside picnics he was always close at hand to fetch and carry for her. Margaret would even occasionally say, 'Shall we take a swim?' Then she would gently slide into the sea and swim about, still smoking a cigarette in her distinctive holder. Back on the beach, Bindon entertained her with his jokes and stories, and she still appeared genuinely fascinated by his background, his working-class accent and his use of cockney rhyming slang.

Margaret caught Bindon stark naked when he was posing on the beach for US photographer Richard Avedon. The princess had suddenly appeared on the scene with her lady-in-waiting and Colin Tennant, all of them deep in conversation. As Margaret looked up, she was confronted by the full-frontal Bindon. Then she gave a little smile and walked off. Her decorum saved red faces all round, but no one present that day had any idea that Bindon and Margaret had been seeing each other regularly in London.

On New Year's Eve 1975, Colin Tennant organised a huge party for everyone on Mustique. Bindon, Vicki and the princess attended along with Dana Gillespie, Mick Jagger, his partner Jerry Hall and Roxy Music star Bryan Ferry. Special food was flown on to the island, and there was a calypso band. During the bash, Margaret danced the Gay Gordons and the Lancers with Bindon. Later, she joined in sing-songs and even sang a solo for the guests. 'It was a magic evening,' Vicki later recalled. 'Colin spared no expense and we all enjoyed ourselves. The princess joined

Chapter Seven

in everything. When she sang, she had a lovely clear voice. John loved dancing with her because she was so good at it.'

And the princess summed up Bindon in one word: 'Fabulous.'

As the group sat around a table overlooking the beach for yet another meal with Margaret, someone leaned towards Bindon and said, 'Ma'am knows about your advantage in life and would really like to see it.' Ever the actor, Bindon didn't hesitate to respond to the request. He jumped up and, with Margaret and her lady-in-waiting in tow, began walking along the beach. Then he stopped about twenty yards from the lunch party, unzipped his flies and took out his flaccid penis which hung a full twelve inches down the side of one leg. Vicki Hodge and others watched from a distance as the princess examined it rather like a fossil. Everyone gasped. Bindon had a smile on his face but said nothing. After a few minutes, they all returned to the table. 'I've seen bigger,' said the lady-in-waiting.

'You may have seen bigger,' Bindon replied. 'But you don't know how well I use it.'

But, as Bindon's friend says, this was all a façade. 'That was all bollocks to disguise the fact that John had been seeing Margaret in London. She already knew all about his tackle!'

Bindon always refused to discuss Margaret with Vicki. Another of Bindon's oldest friends recalled, 'The last person John would tell was Vicki. She would have flogged it to a tabloid in seconds.' Bindon knew from his encounters with Margaret back in London that he needed to keep his trap shut. 'You don't mess with the royal family,' he told one friend.

123

Despite their best attempts, however, within weeks of the couple returning to London, Fleet Street was rife with rumours of an affair between Bindon and Princess Margaret. Everyone knew Margaret had an enormous sexual charisma, and people who had met her in the flesh were often instantly dazzled. She undoubtedly found such colourful characters as Bindon attractive, and she had unashamedly encouraged him. One of John Bindon's oldest friends told this author that Bindon cracked many jokes about how 'I gave her one', but he refused to elaborate. 'He just wouldn't say another word about what really happened between them.'

Greg Hodal confirmed, 'It was all very hush-hush and John didn't talk about it openly. He was very careful. We just knew about an affair with Princess Margaret. Don't forget that Vicki was still legally married at the time and the shame on the royal family would have been too much to bear.'

One of Bindon's relatives says she was in a flat some years after his trips to Mustique when one of his oldest friends, Richard Goodall, asked him, 'Did you actually give Princess Margaret one?'

'We were just sitting having a drink,' she explained, 'and Bindon said, "Of course I fucked PM, but I couldn't get it up her. Because I was too fuckin' big. She couldn't take it. I was too big." He refused to say anything more.'

Vince Chowles had a lengthy relationship with one of Bindon's lovers and insisted to this author that Bindon told his girlfriend he did sleep with Princess Margaret. 'He kept it very quiet. He didn't shout about it. He told his girlfriend he'd be locked up for life if he started talking about it.'

Chapter Seven

Not long after Bindon's return to London, *Daily Mail* gossip columnist Nigel Dempster carried a thinly disguised denial from the princess saying she had never met him. Dempster insisted that her Scotland Yard detective had recognised Bindon immediately on Mustique and ensured there was no possibility of an embarrassing situation. 'That's all bollocks,' Bindon told a friend at the time. 'Thank God they don't know half the truth of it.' He assured his friend he would respect the princess's privacy because 'she's a fine person and doesn't deserve any aggro'.

His old friend and former adversary Joe Pyle said many years later, 'I know John was offered loads of money to tell what really happened when he was with Princess Margaret, but he never would. He thought she was a lovely person and he said he'd never do that to her because he had too much respect for her.'

Princess Margaret continued to visit the Gasworks with Roddy Llewellyn and her dog in tow after returning from the second Mustique trip, although Bindon later told one friend that she had cooled their own relationship. 'John reckoned PM wasn't too keen on Vicki and that ruined things between them. John was Margaret's court jester and I felt a little bit sad for him because she dropped him like a hot potato after he got back from the second trip with Vicki. But much later he did tell me he slept with her. He said he was looking at her earrings thinking, If they drop off, I could buy the whole mews house!'

About a month after his return to London, Bindon was strolling back round to the mews house from The Star when four smartly dressed men in suits appeared at the end of an alleyway. 'They didn't look like your average muggers,' he later explained.

'Mr Bindon, can you come with us please?' one of them asked.

Bindon instantly knew who the men were — MI5 officers. 'They were too smart and posh for the filth,' he recalled. 'This was the heavy mob, so I went quietly.' He climbed in the back of a black Rover coupé and sat between two of the men. As the car drove out of the end of the mews, a police car moved aside to let them through. 'They'd blocked off the fuckin' mews to make sure no one saw what they were up to,' Bindon later told his friend Fred Hayes.

During a forty-minute drive around west and central London, the men in suits explained a few basic rules to Bindon. 'They made it clear that he'd be dragged into the Tower if he muttered a word about his fling with PM,' recalled Hayes.

After being dropped back at the mews house, Bindon headed straight out for a stiff drink, but decided he'd be better off back in his home manor of Fulham. He knew that he'd just crossed swords with the most powerful people in the land and he wanted to avoid any comeback. 'This was more scary than any villains. These people have real power and if they say "off with his head", then that's it, I'm for the chop,' he told one friend that night.

Another of Bindon's oldest criminal associates told this author, 'Bindon was freaked out by that visit from the spooks and he swore then that he would never reveal what happened with the princess.'

Fred Hayes has never forgotten Bindon's face when he

Chapter Seven

walked in for a pint that same evening. 'He came straight into The Britannia and said to me he was well worried, so draw your own conclusions from that. John was really shaken by that visit from the spook squad. Once you interfere with the royal family, things can go badly wrong. No doubt Bindon would have got a lot of money if he'd sold the story, but he knew it wasn't worth it.'

Bindon told Hayes he had a copy of the 'Enjoy Cocaine' photo of him and Princess Margaret, but he had burned it in the fireplace when he got home the night he was 'spoken to'. Fred's mother Nora also had a word with Bindon that night in The Britannia. 'John told me that he'd never talk about it, not for millions,' she later recalled.

But another of Bindon's many criminal associates says that Bindon admitted a number of times that Princess Margaret smoked cannabis in Mustique. 'Bindon said Margaret loved a bit of puff and there was plenty of it on Mustique. She even got him to get her some puff when they saw each other in London. Then Bindon got that serious nasty fuckin' visit by the spook squad and it stopped him talking about it. He clammed up after that. He got threatened in no uncertain terms by that other firm. They blocked the fuckin' road off with normal cops and then took him in the car for a chat. We all know it was MI5.'

Senior Scotland Yard detective George Mould had many later dealings with Bindon, and he insisted to this author that Bindon informed him he had been told to keep quiet about his relationship with Princess Margaret. 'He said we'd never know the truth,' explained Mould. 'And I believed him.' Mould later got a visit from MI5 who were worried that nothing about PM and Bindon should ever leak out.

And one source very close to Princess Margaret's staff at Kensington Palace told this author, 'The Royals have always referred to having sex has "having a ding-dong", and we all knew about Bindon's ding-dongs at KP; but he wasn't the only man in her life by any means. I was told that her staff regularly smelled pot being smoked, but it wasn't our job to point out to PM that she was breaking the law. She enjoyed a lot of ding-dongs with a number of men. So what?'

In 1977, John Bindon appeared at the London Bankruptcy Court facing tax debts of £4,692. He was said to have assets at the time of £272 and the court heard that Bindon's troubles had begun back in the late 1960s when he had earned a rumoured £20,000 from his new career as an actor, but hadn't put any money aside to pay tax. 'I blew it all on the good life – holidays, women and drink,' he later explained. Incredibly, Bindon never had a bank account, let alone an accountant. 'That was typical John,' recalled one old friend. 'He lived for today and didn't give a toss for the future.' But by the time the Inland Revenue started chasing him, his acting career had slowed down. The revenue had earlier even tried to declare him bankrupt in 1973. 'But I changed addresses to get away,' Bindon told one friend.

He even made a point of telling the *Daily Mail* that he was back living with his mother and father in Fulham, although in truth he still had the house in Chesham Mews as a bolt-hole. A few minor acting roles appeared on the horizon, but it was never going to be enough to keep the

Chapter Seven

proverbial wolf from the door. Typically, Bindon insisted, 'I've learned my lesson. I've got myself an accountant and will try and put cash away to pay the tax man in future.' But it was all a brave front. Bindon was in desperate need of a substantial financial injection and remained prepared to take work from *any* side of the water.

So when, in the summer of 1977, his show-business pal Peter Grant, manager of Led Zeppelin, offered him the chance to work on the group's next tour of America, he jumped at the chance. As tour manager Richard Cole explained many years later, 'It wasn't exactly big money and Grant really wanted Bindon as his bodyguard more than anything else, but it was a regular pay packet and that's what John desperately needed at the time.'

It was a perfect escape route for Bindon who was anxious to get out of London while the whole Princess Margaret business cooled down. In recent months he had become paranoid that he wasn't going to get any decent acting work following that sinister visit from the MI5 spooks.

Richard Cole and band members Jimmy Page, Robert Plant and the late John Bonham flew out from London to New York on a BA flight and then went straight to Texas on a private 707 jet specially chartered for the tour. Peter Grant was running so late he rented his own Learjet just to catch up with the rest of the tour party in Dallas. 'He turned up with Bindon,' explained Cole, 'and that was that. Bindon was already known by some of the band. They'd met him before at a launch party in Covent Garden a few months earlier. Bonham loved hanging out with him, but the rest were more wary of him.'

Zeppelin members Page and Plant were clearly not

happy to have such an obvious wild card on board. Cole explained, 'The group had their own US police officer who always ensured we had local police-department protection, and we were never actually told what Bindon was up to. I think he was really there just as Peter's sidekick. He wouldn't have got more than a few hundred quid a week, but he did get to travel by private jet and hang out with the world's most famous rock stars,' recalled Cole.

It soon became obvious Grant saw John Bindon as an excuse to get away with a lot of liberties. 'Peter used Bindon as his shield, although the first ten days of the tour were pretty uneventful, just lots of getting in and out of stretch limos and flying around the country in a private 707,' explained Cole. 'When Zeppelin were in town, everything was on tap – and I mean *everything*.' Bindon knew all about drugs by now because many of his old mates back in west London had graduated from bank robberies to drug deals as they were a lot safer than going across the pavement. 'Bindon considered cannabis acceptable and used it as a way of keeping calm, but all the other heavier drugs were out of bounds. So, when he saw all the mountains of coke and other stuff on open display during the Zeppelin tour, it must have taken his breath away. Initially Bindon was great value for money, and everything seemed to be going smoothly. When we got to New Orleans, he got me out of the shit when a coke dealer tried to run me over during an argument. I'd got the cuff of my trousers caught in the bumpers of his car and thank God Bindon was around. The guy stopped the car and Bindon grabbed the keys and threw them down the drain. We were in the middle of Bourbon Street at the time and

Chapter Seven

the guy took one look at Bindon and just ran off. I could have been shot at if it hadn't been for Bindon that day.'

Bindon found rock tour attitudes quite an eye-opener. 'We just took our pick of women,' said Cole. 'And it took Bindon a while to appreciate the laid-back atmosphere of it all.' When one group member 'arrogantly' ordered Cole and Bindon to get him some action, they went into the front row at a concert and found six girls, put them in a limousine and then on to a plane to New York with the band member in question. 'But before they left we told the girls if they uttered one word to the band member we'd throw them off the plane, so they never said a word. He was so annoyed we were ordered to send them back home on the next flight.'

By the time the band and their entourage arrived in San Francisco, the tour seemed to be running smoothly once again. 'John was still like a fish out of water in some ways, but he was keeping Peter entertained so it wasn't harming anyone and the band were tolerating his presence by this stage.'

In fact, the Zeppelin visit to the States was eventually branded one of the most riotous tours in rock history. Trouble flared in San Francisco when Peter Grant's ten-year-old son tried to remove an ornate wooden plaque with the band's name from their dressing-room door. Security guard Jim Matzorkis told the boy he couldn't have it and cuffed him on the back of the head. Led Zeppelin drummer John 'Bonzo' Bonham, who had left the stage during an acoustic number, saw what was going on and demanded Matzorkis apologise. Then Bonham decided for good measure to kick the terrified security guard in the goolies. 'He fell to the floor like a sack of melons,' Cole remembered.

When Grant – formerly a professional heavyweight wrestler – heard his boy had been hit, he was so outraged he went in search of the injured guard with Richard Cole and 'bodyguard' John Bindon. Matzorkis had gone into hiding, so the pair tricked legendary promoter Bill Graham into revealing where he was by promising there wouldn't be any trouble. Graham took Grant to a trailer where Matzorkis was hiding, and Grant went inside with Bindon 'for a chat'. Graham later recalled that, 'Peter blasted Jim in the face. I tried to stand between them, but Grant forced me out of the trailer and locked the door. My man said, "Bill! Bill! Help me!" Matzorkis worked his way to the door while they were hitting him. His face was soon a bloody mess.'

Richard Cole – standing outside the trailer with one of his security staff – claims Graham then sent in an army of twenty guards to rescue Matzorkis. 'I saw these guys coming and I picked up a piece of aluminium tubing from a table umbrella and fought them,' said Cole. 'A lot of the guys had these special gloves with lead and sand in them.' Cole chased Graham employee Bob Barsotti across the green and over a fence before smashing him in the face with the pipe. Then local carpenter Jim Downey cracked a joke about twenty-five-stone Grant's waistline. An outraged Bindon immediately knocked Downey out with a single punch. Others then started banging Downey's head against a concrete wall.

Later, Zeppelin guitarist Jimmy Page insisted Grant, Cole and Bindon had acted in self-defence. 'I'll tell you

Chapter Seven

there was a team of guys there with sand in their gloves,' said Page. 'It was a very hairy scene. If somebody hits you, you hit them back – it's self-defence, innit?'

When tempers cooled, the Zeppelin entourage returned to their hotel to plan their next move. They knew they risked arrest, but had an ace in the hole as the band was due to play another sell-out show the following afternoon. The band's lawyer then called Bill Graham with a veiled threat that Zeppelin wouldn't play unless a waiver was signed to indemnify them from any subsequent police action. Graham's lawyer assured him anything signed under duress would not hold up in court. Tensions ran high the next morning when the band arrived at the Oakland Stadium for the second show. Half an hour before Zeppelin were due to play, Bill Graham signed the waiver and the show went ahead, but Bindon and the rest of the band's team departed the stadium at high speed afterwards. Later, lawyers filed charges to have Peter Grant, John Bonham, Richard Cole and John Bindon arrested.

At the hotel, one of Zeppelin's security guards, an ex-police officer with a friend in the local SWAT team, informed them that Bindon and the others were about to be arrested. 'When we heard what was happening, we phoned to say we were coming down to the police station peacefully,' said Cole. 'Otherwise it could have been a terrible mess if they'd gone in shooting.' Matzorkis and two other Graham staff members then filed a $2 million damages suit against Grant, Bonham, Cole and Bindon.

Zeppelin's lawyers eventually agreed to pay an undisclosed amount to Graham's staff. That final Oakland show turned out to be Led Zeppelin's last performance in

America, and not long afterwards the group stopped performing altogether. In court at Oakland, California, guilty pleas to assault charges were filed on behalf of Bindon, Grant, Bonham and Cole. Bindon was given a suspended sixty-day jail sentence and fined £300 in his absence. The others were fined £200 each.

As Richard Cole explained, 'Bill Graham owned San Francisco and he was capable of pulling any stroke you could thing of. We had fucked him over and he was out to get us. Graham was behind our arrest. He orchestrated it. We were lucky to get out of there in one piece.

Bindon thought he would be happy to get back to the relative peace and sanity of London after the battles of San Francisco. But there were clashes of a different nature awaiting him: his relationship with Vicki Hodge was about to spark more bitter partings and equally passionate reconciliations.

Girls in the smart Chelsea set had long since dubbed Vicki the Flying Nun because of her fiery way of dealing with love rivals. She clobbered one in a busy street, and once even hurled a milk bottle at a woman. As Vicki herself later admitted, 'I never turned a blind eye to his affairs with other women. I would always go round banging on doors, causing terrible scenes and bopping the girls. My whirlwind acts of vengeance got me such a reputation that the girls in Chelsea became terrified. Some of them still are.'

But then, Vicki always had good reason to be jealous during her many turbulent years with Bindon. 'He had endless affairs. There were the famous names, and in

Chapter Seven

between them came a procession of hairdressers, film-set girls and West End slags.'

So it was no surprise when, on 27 June 1978, Bindon's womanising ways hit the headlines in the *Daily Express*'s William Hickey column, which reported that Bunny Club PR girl Serena Williams had broken up with her soccer hard-man lover Big Malcolm Allison and taken up with another tough guy called John Bindon. Bindon made no attempt to deny the story and even told one of the column's reporters, 'I bumped into Serena in The Water Rat pub in the King's Road, Chelsea, and we've been dating for about two months. I like her very, very much. But marriage has never been discussed. I'm just trying to improve my mind.'

Vicki Hodge was also approached by the paper and said her love affair with Bindon was over. 'There are no hard feelings. I wish them all the happiness in the world.' Meanwhile, Serena Williams insisted to the paper that her only domestic companion at home was her parrot!

But Vicki Hodge wasn't going to let Bindon off the hook that easily. By August 1978, she informed the London *Evening News* that her estranged husband Ian Heath had been in touch since reading about the alleged end of her relationship with Bindon. She brazenly told the paper, 'I think Ian would like me back. He asked me how I felt when my romance with John ended. Of course, I was quite upset. Ten years is such a long time and you have to take a deep breath and start all over again. What I do resent is the vulgar way it ended – John might have replaced me with someone with a bit more class. Ian has invited me to join him for a holiday in Germany, probably in September. We've never divorced because neither of us ever wanted to. In spite of everything, I like being married to him. It's a security to know there is always someone in the background who cares.'

As one of Bindon's closest friends at the time later explained, 'John went fuckin' crazy when he read what Vicki had said. She knew precisely how to press his buttons and we all knew they'd soon be back together.'

The truth was that Vicki had been devastated by Bindon's affair with Serena. On one occasion she spotted them outside a Chelsea pub and her emotions got the better of her. She allegedly stormed up to them and socked Serena in the eye. 'I always think that, if you really love a man, you should be prepared to fight for him,' she said afterwards.

But Serena wasn't that easily put off. Vicki claimed that she later stormed into Serena's flat and caught him in bed with her. Vicki then threw all Bindon's belongings – which he kept at her flat – into a bag and drove round to Serena's place on the King's Road. When Serena answered the door, Vicki dumped the bag on the hall floor and screamed at her, 'If you want to go to bed with him, perhaps you'd like to do his washing and ironing, too.' Then she walked out.

Vicki later admitted it was at that moment she believed Serena might really be in love with Bindon and not just flirting with him. 'But I was very angry that she could come between a couple who'd been together for so long. Everybody knew John was my old man and I was his old lady.'

Later, Serena Williams strongly denied Vicki's claims that she had caught her and Bindon in bed. 'Vicki did not catch

Chapter Seven

John and I in bed. Apart from anything else, she could not get into my house without my consent because of the security system.'

By the end of the summer of 1978, Bindon had apparently returned to Vicki Hodge, who immediately 'celebrated' by phoning her favourite gossip columnist at the *Daily Express*: 'We've had an absolutely lovely, passionate reunion and we've decided to get on with our lives together. John and I have been close for ten years. Everyone has a seven-year itch. He just had a ten-year one.' She added hopefully, 'It's domestic bliss and I hope it's for keeps.'

It was a real-life soap saga which promised to run and run.

Chapter Eight

Ask any copper in F Division – west London – back then and he would tell you the area was rife with villains. 'There were the hardcore Irish over in Shepherds Bush and the whole mix clashed in Hammersmith, right in the middle. Fulham was about old-fashioned villainy as opposed to murder and stuff like that, which we got more of in Shepherds Bush,' explained the head of F Division, Detective Chief Superintendent George Mould. 'There were professional families in Fulham, moneylenders and stuff like that, and they all liked to think they were thriving and that we didn't know what they were all up to.'

So it was hardly surprising that illegal after-hours clubs and bars thrived down discreet alleyways and in dingy basements across the manor. One favourite haunt was the Ranelagh Yacht Club, a seedy hole-in-the-wall establishment where everything but boats was discussed. It was a clever name because when Bindon and his pals referred to 'going down the Yacht Club' it sounded like somewhere you went for an afternoon out on the river. Nothing could have been further from the truth – the club was located under a rundown archway below the District line tube track, just a stone's throw from the river Thames and Putney Bridge.

As one of Bindon's lovers, beautiful model Mona explained many years later, 'I was so impressed that John was a member of a yacht club. It sounded so posh and I thought to myself, This guy is much more upmarket than I thought. But then we walked down this grim alleyway and through a tatty door in a wall and ended up having a drink in a cigarette-burned cubicle with damp, red-velvet covers, and there wasn't another girl in sight.' When she first walked in the Yacht Club, Mona had been in the newspapers quite a lot on account of her modelling, so all the regulars gave her the once-over. 'It sort of impressed me. They were all very polite and respectful, as was John in their company.'

The Yacht Club was particularly popular with all 'the chaps' in the afternoon because back then pubs closed at three o'clock and didn't reopen until early evening. Another regular described the club: 'It looked like an abandoned building from the outside and in some ways it was a joke. It was very overgrown outside but was not near the road so whatever happened inside could not be heard.'

The Yacht Club was a complete eye-opener to young, innocent, middle-class Mona. 'Naturally I was in my shortest mini, but I was very straight and I suppose I was one of John's trophy girls.' Mona was introduced by

Chapter Eight

Bindon to a variety of characters including his pals Johnny Gillette, Roy Dennis, Bobby Buckley and Alan Stanton. Then there were two other villains called Lennie and Joe, one of whom had shot his leg off in a bank robbery. 'Alan Stanton and Buckley were discussing a robbery in front of me, but they told me afterwards they reckoned I didn't look like the kind of girl who'd land them in trouble so they just carried on,' said Mona. 'I never asked too many questions because villains hate that as it makes them feel vulnerable and they don't like giving information away. I was also quite shy so I was quiet, and I was a very good drinker, which they also liked.'

Mona frequently encountered two John Bindons during her on-off relationship with him. 'One was courting me and a complete gentleman, while the other was a hardened criminal quite prepared to do anything if necessary. But John satisfied a need within me to do something a bit crazy. I was bored and I suppose I was looking for the excitement of being with a villain.'

All the regulars in the Yacht Club remained on their best behaviour when gorgeous Mona was around, but it was a different story for Bindon's American actor pal Greg Hodal, who had first got to know the Yacht Club when he was staying with him in Belgravia. 'I noticed it started getting a much heavier atmosphere in the middle of 1978. It seemed to be close to boiling point down there and I remember a couple of times having to go out with some kind of protection – a knife – because John was worried something might happen. Sometimes the opposition from the other side of the river were in the Yacht Club trying to wind things up. It was really just about staring people down. But the Yacht Club was considered a neutral place which was, in a way, still up for grabs.'

Another popular after-hours drinking club was J Arthur's (cockney rhyming slang for 'wank') on the King's Road. It was run by Freddie Foreman at the time and, because of his south-London origins, other well-known faces such as Kenny Baker and the Arif family had become regular visitors from across the river. Another even less welcome face from south London was a tall, swarthy, minor-league villain called John Darke. Darke didn't knock round with these other names. He lived in Tulse Hill and had another house in Elmer's End, near Crystal Palace. Darke and his associates liked to call themselves the Wild Bunch. Foreman wasn't impressed. 'Fuckin' pathetic name for a bunch of right cowboys,' he recalled. Darke soon informed other regulars in J Arthur's he wasn't impressed by the so-called professionals from Fulham, including alleged hard man John Bindon. One of Bindon's oldest mates later explained, 'Darke seemed jealous of John's acting, his girlfriends and his reputation as a solid hitter. But then a lot of the villains were a bit confused by John at times. They couldn't really work out where he was coming from.'

But there was no doubt where John Arthur Darke came from. In 1954, at the age of sixteen, he had managed two escapes from remand homes and a third from a court's detention room. At nineteen he had even made the front page of various newspapers by escaping from Pentonville in bare feet after being jailed for conspiracy to rob, possession of a shotgun and cartridges, car theft and armed robbery. In 1964 he was jailed for armed robbery, and in

Chapter Eight

1974 he served another term for unlawful wounding. South-London detective Terry Babbidge knew him well. 'Darke was a nasty piece of work. He liked to think he knew the police and could buy us off. He was scum.'

At the time, Babbidge was looking closely at Darke in connection with a number of serious crimes, but Darke had managed to get the police off his back by providing them with information about a bank robbery in Paddington, which led to the arrest of two very well-known blaggers. 'You could say Darke was under our wing at the time, although I didn't trust the guy,' says Babbidge.

But worse still, police tapping Darke's phone in 1977 had stumbled upon a murder he had committed. 'It came up when we heard him tell his wife he'd killed a West Indian fella in a pub,' explained Babbidge. 'Stabbed him to death. On the phone, he was telling his wife what to do with his bloodstained clothing. Based on that, we planned to eventually arrest Darke for murder.'

But then Darke got a tip-off from a police contact that he was about to be pinched and went on his toes. Ironically, he eventually gave himself up, only to be acquitted because of a lack of evidence. According to Babbidge, Darke then swapped the risks of going across the pavement for a more lucrative career trafficking drugs. Police even put his south-London scrap yard under secret surveillance. 'Darke was dealing in heroin and cocaine. He had teams of runners selling it. He was a middle-brow crim, not top drawer, but he was certainly earning decent money.'

Officially, Darke called himself a van-hire merchant, but his workplace also included the pubs and clubs of south

London, especially Brixton. Many of these 'business deals' involved protection money as well as drugs, but he was so desperate to get into the big league he was often careless about where he got his drugs from. Sometimes he even used an underworld informant to help him steal drugs from other gangs. He was renowned as someone who would do business with anyone. In the summer of 1978, he was even questioned by police about the burning down of a Surrey country club and an east-London pub in a suspected insurance fraud. 'He was certainly a very, very busy boy,' says Babbidge. He was also running a lucrative scam as a receiver of lorry loads from hijackings. 'You could claim insurance if the loads remained missing for more than twenty-four hours, so that meant they'd nick anything and then share the claim. The villains were working with the lorry drivers.'

But John Darke was playing a dangerous game. On the one hand, he appeared to be a successful career criminal; on the other hand, he was feeding the Flying Squad with titbits that he thought would keep them off his back. 'It was common knowledge that Darke had a price on his head. In the sort of circles he mixed in, it was only a matter of time before someone got him,' explained detective Babbidge.

In October 1978, Freddie Foreman was in J Arthur's with his wife and two other couples. 'John Darke and his pals turned up and got very heavy after the club barman – a New Zealander – accidentally knocked over their drinks. I offered to buy them new drinks and Darke said he wanted the kid sorted. We had a bit of a confrontation but they backed down. I didn't like Darke's style one bit. He came into my place expecting to get a lot of respect and none of

Chapter Eight

us gave a fuck about him. He was just one of many small-timers trying to make a name for themselves.'

A few days after this incident, Darke upset Foreman further by starting a fight in another one of his clubs, the Ellelsly in Crystal Palace. 'He went and chinned Little Legs Gifford who was in partnership with me in a car showroom over in the Walworth Road. It was completely out of order.' Foreman ended up sorting out Darke himself. 'It turned into a bit of a row and we threw Darke and his mates down the stairs after a straightener. I'd had enough of him and his mates.' Foreman was so furious he seriously contemplated 'finishing off' Darke.

A few days later John Bindon strolled into his Crystal Palace club with the Dennis brothers, a robber called Ray Johnson and some other well-known Fulham faces. 'What you doing in this neck of the woods?' asked Foreman.

'Heard you had a row with Johnny Darke last week,' said Bindon.

'That's right. He took a liberty with Little Legs and chinned him and that was it. He's barred up here,' responded a wary Foreman.

'Well, he used to say he was your big pal, Freddie,' said Bindon in a cold, indifferent tone.

Foreman was one of the most powerful faces in London at the time, and he sensed this conversation was heading in a dangerous direction. Neither man said anything for a few moments. Bindon broke the silence by leaning down and pulling a huge bowie knife out from the side of his cowboy boots. 'Well I've got this for him.'

Ever the seasoned professional, Foreman didn't bat an eyelid and turned towards Bindon and the others. 'Far as

I'm concerned, lads, it's open season on that prat. If you want to go to work on him, it's up to you. You've got a licence to do him if you want.'

Foreman smiled before looking down at Bindon's flashy cowboy boots. 'Any time you want a pair, let me know, Freddie,' said Bindon.

Foreman laughed. 'They're not really my cup of tea.'

A few weeks later, John Bindon popped into the Ranelagh Yacht Club for an afternoon tipple. Inside it was buzzing with at least sixty other faces, including John Darke. As one other drinker later explained, 'Darke was a wrong 'un surrounded by little mugs, and trouble was in the air.' That said, Darke's common-law wife Susan later insisted that, 'John was certainly not expecting any trouble when he went to the club. If he had, he would have taken a gun.'

Actor Greg Hodal was with Bindon that afternoon. 'We were upstairs when Johnny Darke showed up,' he recalled. 'At first nothing happened and everything seemed to smooth over. In fact, after two hours it was so sweet I decided to take off to see my girlfriend who lived nearby and had promised to cook me dinner. My last memory of John was him looking extremely relaxed.'

But trouble was brewing. Nora Hayes later recalled that Darke and his associates had walked into her pub earlier that same day 'looking for trouble'. 'My husband told our boys not to go to the Yacht Club that night. We knew something was up.'

Back inside the Yacht Club, a scuffle had started between a female customer called Maureen Brady and barmaid Anna Mulligan over a boyfriend of Brady's. As Bindon

Chapter Eight

wandered up to the toilets, he and a few others had a bit of a giggle about the feuding women. Then he turned and caught a cold, hard stare from John Darke leaning on the bar opposite. A couple of minutes later, Bindon reappeared to see his close pal Roy Dennis being challenged by Darke. Suddenly a knife was glistening in Darke's hand and he was slashing at Roy Dennis's face, neck and forehead. Then he plunged the blade into Dennis's back.

'What the fuck's going on here?' screamed Bindon and his close mate Alan Stanton, who was hobbling around the club on crutches because of a broken leg. Bindon steamed in to try and restrain Darke and was immediately stabbed in the back by someone else. At this point three of Darke's associates called Begbe, Bohm and Galbraith tried to stop anyone else intervening. Bindon fell to the floor and Darke sat astride him and stabbed him in the neck, head, chest and face. 'He'd already stuck me in the chest,' Bindon remembered, 'and I was pleading for my life. I got up and thought he'd done for me.' It was then Bindon struck out at Darke.

Bindon later admitted he didn't know how many times he stuck his knife into Darke, but said, 'Two or three times that I know.'

Ernie Begbe naturally had a different take on proceedings. 'There were a lot of people moving about and I heard someone shout "Darkie!" and I heard a crash. I saw Darke on his back on a table. Then he sprang up straight away and moved towards the side of the room.'

Begbe later said he then asked Darke what was going on and Darke told him to get off. 'After a few seconds two big blokes came up and rushed straight into John [Darke]. They were both going at him with a knife.'

However, Bindon later recalled, 'After Darke cut my throat I heard a scream and Lennie Osborne appeared with a machete and slashed Darke across the spine. I lunged at Darke and stabbed him in the chest, but if I hadn't done that he would have come back at me and finished me off. Everyone was running around, screaming. One of them got a bottle of vodka over his head. Nice way to spend a Monday afternoon.'

After Bindon had stabbed Darke, he approached injured Roy Dennis and hobbling Alan Stanton and asked them what he should do. 'I remember Alan was sitting in one of the cubicles and he just said, "You gotta do what you gotta do."'

Stanton claimed years later, 'Everyone was sticking the knife into Darke and John was the best person to put up for the job.' But, whatever the truth of the matter, John Bindon was terribly wounded. He thought he was about to die. As he later told police, 'I thought Darke had done me and that's why I went for him. He was playing with me. It was like a hostage situation. I was trying to talk him out of it, saying, "What are you doing, Darkie? You are going to kill me." He had already stuck me in the chest and I was pleading for my life. There was something strange about him, as if he was enjoying it, wielding the knife round slowly and saying to me, "Bindon, you're not so big now." He was like an animal. I'm a strong man but I felt myself going weak. No one made a move to help me and people were holding back others with knives.'

As Bindon fell bleeding from at least two stab wounds, Darke once again moved in for the kill; Bindon later claimed somewhat theatrically that he said to Darke that,

Chapter Eight

if he was going to die, then at least he should be allowed to die on his feet. Darke then stepped back to allow this last request – and fell dying himself, his spine severed by that blow from Osborne's machete.

Ernie Begbe later alleged that, as he went to try and get help, one of the men – the one with the knife (presumably Bindon) – asked him if he was Darke's friend and then slashed him across the face, slicing off part of his nose. 'Blood was pouring out of my face. I expected to see John [Darke] fighting when I got back, but he was still on his back.' As Bindon's associate Lennie Osborne was helping him out of the club, he saw Darke lying, knees bent, on the floor near the fire-escape exit.

Begbe and Galbraith then carried Darke out of the bar, with another man helping them down the steps. Begbe explained, 'George and this other guy tried to give John Darke the kiss of life. I think I gave him a thump on the heart a couple of times.' Stabbed more than nine times, Darke was taken to hospital where he was found to be dead on arrival.

Outside the Yacht Club, Bindon's pals were determined to get him away from the premises before the police turned up, so a local character called Mickey Sullivan drove him and Stanton just a few hundred yards to 166 New King's Road where the Hayes family – landlords of The Britannia – lived in a second-floor flat. Nora Hayes takes up the story: 'I was cooking the dinner when there was a knock on the door and they dragged John in. He'd collapsed outside my front door and was bleeding very badly. "He's been stabbed," yelled Mickey Sullivan. "Get a fuckin' doctor."'

Bindon struggled to reach an armchair before grabbing

the phone and calling Vicki Hodge at her nearby flat in Bishop's Park. 'This is it, babe, I'm dying,' he told her on the phone. 'Get some money together, put a couple of shirts in a bag and come round.'

As Nora Hayes later explained, 'John's heart was visible through his shirt which was pouring with blood from his neck, and one of his mates was sitting there with all his fingers hanging off. It wasn't a pretty sight!'

Vicki Hodge raced round in her Mini Cooper with £100 to pay for the doctor. She nearly fainted when she first saw Bindon. 'He'd been stabbed in the heart, in the back, in the eye, in the throat and in the testicles. Every time his heart beat, blood shot out of his shirt. I tore up my white skirt and made it into bandages.'

Typically, Bindon begged her, 'Don't take my boots off. Let me die with them on.' Then, as Nora remembered, he started saying, 'Get me a joint, get me a joint!'

'All the heavyweight villains were circling that room,' recalled Vicki. "What can we do? We gotta do something? It's all over. He's gonna die here." It was chaos.'

Then Bindon yelled, 'Get me to Ireland where my mum comes from!' Calls went out from London to Dublin to get Bindon looked after.

Downstairs, Roy Dennis's brother Gerry had already driven off to get some more clean clothes from Bindon's parents' home at nearby Sullivan Court. 'I eventually helped pull off John's cowboy boots,' remembered Nora, 'and we washed the blood off them. The knife he'd used on Darke was still in them.'

Alan Stanton grabbed a bottle of Scotch from a sideboard and started pouring it down Bindon's throat to

Chapter Eight

try and quell the pain. 'We also stuffed some tranquillisers in his mouth to try and slow his blood down so he didn't bleed internally,' explained Nora.

Nora had just taken off Bindon's shirt and other clothes and was putting them in the dustbin in the kitchen when Stanton screamed at her. 'No way. You mustn't do that, love. It's the first place the filth will look.' She then handed a plastic bag with the blood-splattered clothes to Vicki.

'I was new to this sort of thing,' explained Nora, 'so I just did as I was told.' She wrapped Bindon in a red blanket she had in the flat so that when the blood came soaking through it wouldn't be so obvious. 'John was in the flat for maybe half an hour. He said to me, "How long will it take to get to Ireland?", and I said forty minutes. Then the doctor came and said to boil a kettle and he sterilised some needles and started sewing John up. We'd known and trusted that doctor for years and he'd been in to mend a few others in his time. We kept feeding John whiskey and the silly bugger was smoking a big fat joint the whole time. It seemed to calm him down.'

Outside the Hayes's front window, sirens were blaring as the police raced down the New King's Road towards the Yacht Club. Inside the flat, a hobbling Alan Stanton grabbed a mop and bucket and began frantically cleaning up the blood-soaked floor.

Back at the Yacht Club itself, dozens of customers were cleaning and polishing everything to remove any potential evidence before the police arrived. Sixty members had seen the fight, but not one of them intended to grass anyone else up. Most vanished within minutes, as did the membership book they had all signed. Less than a hundred feet away, two well-known faces called Alfie Gerrard and Gerry Callaghan were throwing many of the weapons used in the fight into the Thames. As Joey Pyle later explained, 'They had to get rid of any evidence. If it had been my club I would have done the same.'

At the Hayes's flat, Vicki and Bindon's close friend Lennie Osborne struggled to help Bindon down the stairs to a waiting car being driven by another pal, Johnny Gillette. Bindon was driven with Vicki to Heathrow Airport. He threw his knife out of the car window during the journey. At the Aer Lingus reservations desk, Vicki told the clerk her boyfriend had been injured in a rugby game and had to get home to Dublin so they let him on the plane. 'John had a scarf around him and there was blood seeping through it so he looked weird,' she later recalled. Meanwhile, contacts in the IRA had been called by Bindon's associates in London so that a hideout could be arranged.

Nora Hayes's husband George was secretary of the Yacht Club, and they knew the police would be over to see them sooner rather than later, so they headed for The Britannia. 'The police eventually turned up in the pub to tell us that someone had been murdered at the Yacht Club,' explained Nora. 'We said, "Really? How terrible!" I'll never forget the way the two plod just stood at the bar in their hush puppies. Luckily they didn't even bother to ask us about the flat.'

In another part of Fulham, Greg Hodal was eating dinner with his girlfriend at her home in Wandsworth Bridge Road when somebody knocked on his door. 'This guy said to me, "Listen, we gotta talk to you and you have to come with us." I told my girlfriend I'd be back in a few

Chapter Eight

minutes.' In fact, he was whisked to Heathrow Airport, given a bag filled with papers and cash and told to take a different flight to Dublin. 'I was driven by a couple of mutual friends who should remain nameless to this day,' he explained recently. 'In the car they told me that Darke was dead and John had been spirited off to Ireland, and they needed someone who was not connected to deliver some papers to him the next day.'

Hodal believes that he was picked for his 'mission' because he was not a criminal and had an American passport, which made him much less likely to be spotted by police. 'This was in the middle of the IRA bombing campaign, so being American was a definite advantage.' Once in Dublin, he was told to book a hotel room and wait to be contacted. 'So I called my girlfriend and said, "I'm not going to be back for pudding!"'

Chapter Nine

At the scene of the murder, police were hardly surprised to find most of the evidence of the fight had been cleared up and none of the weapons used were anywhere to be found. Detectives did, however, find a number of cartridge shells hidden behind some panelling inside the Yacht Club, although they didn't seem relevant to the killing of John Darke. They wanted answers to questions. Who wielded the machete that killed Darke? Who else was at the club when the fight broke out and took part? A couple of informants had called in to say that two gangs were warring over the rich pickings of a protection racket, but for the moment the police had no idea what had really happened.

Detective Chief Superintendent George Mould had only recently taken over the notorious F Division. Mould was an upstanding, old-school copper who had joined the Met in 1952 and worked at various nicks all over south and west London. His two biggest claims to fame were as the bag-carrier on the Hanratty murder case and then transcribing the Christine Keeler tapes for the Profumo Inquiry that helped bring down the Tory Government in the early 1960s. His take on his career was modest and low-key: 'I was lucky. I happened to be around at the right place and right time.' Later, Mould helped form the Bomb Squad following IRA outrages in London. Now he was expecting a quieter time in west London.

Mould had just finished supper at his family home in Long Ditton, Surrey, when the phone rang. 'Guv'nor, we've got one,' said the voice of one of his colleagues.

'I knew from that we must have a murder on our hands,' he later recalled. He ordered the officer to send his car and driver. 'I'd never been there, but the Yacht Club was well known to us as the sort of place you'd go to if you wanted to keep your ear to the ground.' It was raining hard that night as Mould was driven in his black police Hillman Hunter to Fulham. 'Initially, you don't know what the hell you've got until you get there,' he later explained. 'We got to the scene and there were lots of people milling around, but there was no scene-of-crime tape back in those days so I had a quick look around just to get a feel for the place. I soon noticed there was lots of blood. Forensic people were dusting and dropping things in plastic bags and there was no sign of the membership book, which was hardly a surprise!'

Mould had a small entourage of officers walking behind him as he stepped inside the club. 'It's like when you see a surgeon in a hospital, I suppose. Everyone was behind me

Chapter Nine

as I walked. The press were being kept well away. The local-paper boys were already there and I expected I'd get a few calls from them later, but for the moment my priority was the murder itself.'

After examining the inside of the club for about twenty minutes, Mould returned to his black Hillman and drove to his office at Hammersmith nick. He ordered his officers to set up an incident room at Fulham Police Station as it was nearer to the scene. 'You have to get your troops together, get hold of pathologists and forensic people, organise the post-mortem and all that sort of thing, so I started ringing around to take various officers off other things as murders take precedence over everything.'

Mould had already heard of John Darke. 'I also knew a few of the names who were thrown up as having been at the club that evening.' Everyone who was at the premises when the police first arrived was detained and told to stay inside the club. Some would eventually be taken back to Fulham Police Station. Everyone – without exception – insisted they had seen nothing and claimed they were in the toilets at the time of the stabbing. 'That did seem a bit strange,' Mould explained, 'but hardly surprising – and remember that the majority of them had already scarpered by the time I got there. The ones who were left were having a right go at us about being kept in the club.'

Mould insisted those still inside the club be held until police had absolute proof of their names and addresses. Then he went to see one of the survivors – Darke's friend Ernie Begbe – at Charing Cross Hospital in the nearby Fulham Palace Road. He refused to say anything.

When one of Mould's junior officers told him that a

character called John Bindon was among the men who had been drinking at the club earlier, Mould said, 'Who the fuck's Bindon?' 'The name meant little to me at that time, but I ordered one of my men to check out any of his antecedents. He was just one of many names we'd have to raid the homes of to see what he had to say.'

Less than half a mile away, Vicki Hodge and Bindon's younger sister Geraldine were now back at her flat trying to destroy all his bloodstained clothes and burn those snakeskin boots in the fire. 'We shredded them first and then burned them,' she later explained. At 5.15 a.m. – less than an hour after they had finally gone to bed – there was a bang at the door. Vicki sprung up believing that perhaps Bindon had come back. 'But it was the police, and they poured in and then dispersed like ants searching through the flat.'

'So where is he?' one officer barked at Vicki.

'Not here. He's not here,' she replied before running off the names of Bindon's other women, making a special point of mentioning Serena Williams. Vicki later claimed there were still bloodstains from Bindon's clothes on the carpet, but the detectives didn't notice them. The embers were still crackling and a lambskin rug, covered with Bindon's blood, was still soaking in the bathtub. 'The fireplace still had the charred remains of all his clothes and those boots. But I wasn't guilty of anything. I was aiding and abetting the man I love. He came to me for help so I gave him help.'

Bindon travelled under his Eire-born mother's maiden name of Monaghan on the 11.55 p.m. Aer Lingus flight EI179 to Dublin, wrapped in Nora Hayes's red blanket,

Chapter Nine

which hid the blood seeping from his gaping wounds. Fortunately, there was no passport control for travellers between the two countries. A secret phone message was conveyed from Dublin to London to announce Bindon's arrival, and warning that the police might be hot on his trail. 'The baby's arrived. Now we're waiting for the afterbirth to arrive,' was the coded message.

At Dublin, Bindon was met by two brothers from a local family called the Dunnes who were to look after him and his escort Lennie Osborne. It later transpired that one of his lungs had collapsed on the flight to Dublin. He was immediately taken to a secret hideout in the nearby Wicklow Mountains. The following day, George Hayes and Bindon's old pal Jimmy Sullivan were dispatched to Dublin to see him. 'My husband looked like a cop in his long cashmere coat with collar and tie,' recalled Nora. 'They went up to the Wicklow Mountains and talked to John about what to do next.'

It was clear to the two men that Bindon was extremely sick, but he insisted he could ride it out. To prove his point, he started doing sit-ups on the floor of the farmhouse where he was hiding. 'When he started doing the sit-ups, it split one of his wounds open and he collapsed. His guts were virtually hanging out of him,' said Nora. Hayes and Sullivan felt they had no choice but to take him to the nearest hospital, otherwise he would have bled to death. They decided to tell the nuns he had been stabbed by the 'filthy British' up north. At St Vincent's Hospital, Irishman George Hayes, tall and imposing and still wearing that long trenchcoat, convinced the nuns he was a policeman and they agreed to give

Bindon immediate treatment. Nora later explained that, 'One of the sisters was humming "Ava Maria" and suddenly Bindon comes round and starts singing it with her at the top of his voice, and she said, "Mr Monaghan, will you please be quiet. What would these two CID officers think if they heard you?" Sullivan and Hayes were pacing up and down the floor nearby. That sort of thing only ever happens in a crazy place like Ireland!'

Hayes advised Bindon to think very carefully about what to do next because, unless he came back of his own accord to London, he would definitely be found guilty if he was ever captured. Sullivan advised him to give himself up, but Bindon wasn't sure and decided to play for a bit more time.

Meanwhile, a few miles away in a Dublin hotel, bemused Californian actor Greg Hodal had got up bright and early to await his instructions from Bindon's associates. Finally, he got the call to go to the hospital with the papers and cash he had brought over the previous day. 'I kinda wandered around the hospital for a little bit and then found a friendly nurse who explained that "Mr Monaghan" was a secret patient but pointed out where he was. I went in and there were drips hanging out of every part of John's body. I told him I had some papers that consisted of a fake passport and other stuff that he might need if he decided to slip back into the UK. John laughed when he saw me, but I couldn't hang around for long because that would have jeopardised his safety, so I left pretty quickly.'

Hodal says that to this day he has never regretted helping his friend. 'My name would have been mud if I'd refused

Chapter Nine

to help. There were a couple of people who fell by the wayside because there was a bit of grassing going on and people losing their bottle, but I was determined to help. It was the least I owed John.'

Back in London, DCS George Mould and his squad of detectives were hearing rumours that Bindon had played a significant role in the murder. Their interest had also been fuelled by his disappearance from the flat he was supposed to be sharing with Vicki Hodge (they had no idea he had been spending most of his time at the house in Chesham Mews). 'We started looking for dodgy doctors who might have attended to him,' Mould later recalled. 'People were beginning to talk about Bindon and the word was that he was seriously injured.' Mould even suspected Bindon might be dead. 'Then I heard a whisper he'd gone to Ireland. People were saying that one of the firms in the club that night had connections with the Provisional IRA through guns and drugs. But there was no actual concrete information so we were just chasing around, assuming he'd gone.'

Mould was surprised when a number of local hoods came out of the woodwork and offered their help. 'I think a lot of them thought this was one they couldn't hide from because of the enormous publicity. They were scared that unless we got our man we might take a lot of them down with him.' However, the police did not yet know specifically what role Bindon had played in the killing of John Darke. Mould was also wary that some of his informants might try and pin the blame on Bindon and turn him into a sacrificial lamb. 'We even heard that another villain had disappeared at exactly the same time as Bindon and he'd been sliced into pieces on a billiard table in another club and then fed to the fishes,' said Mould. 'The main thing was that we were kicking a few doors down by now. Getting search warrants and starting to make headway. We didn't find a lot out, but we were stirring people up. We made another call to Vicki Hodge, advising her to come in to see us rather than being fetched as this could look very nasty for her show-business career. We also spoke to Serena Williams and a lot of local scallywags who'd known Bindon most of his life. Serena Williams was open about having seen Bindon the day of the incident, not that it was particularly relevant to the inquiry.'

When Mould asked Williams if she knew anything about the knife that had been partly used to kill Darke, they got their biggest breakthrough to date. 'She immediately admitted it could be her knife, which Bindon kept in his boot for decorative reasons.'

Bindon was now George Mould's number-one suspect. 'I suppose you could say it was all rather convenient, but everything pointed to Bindon being the killer. Of course, there were a lot of people with knives in that club that night, and they weren't saying anything until they knew which way I was going. But I'd decided Bindon was my man so I stepped up the hunt for him immediately.'

Mould then interviewed a petty crook from the Fulham area who told him that Bindon had definitely gone to Ireland by ferry on the night of the murder. 'Trouble was, he didn't know if he was south or north of the Irish border.' Then Mould remembered that some of the drinkers in the Yacht Club that night had possible IRA

Top: Bindon started off on the wrong foot with South London underworld boss Joey Pyle but the two became great pals.

Above: Legendary criminal Freddie Foreman clashed with Bindon's 'victim' John Darke just weeks before Darke was stabbed to death.

Top: *Vogue* Model Clemmie Simon, whom Bindon rescued from drug dens on many occasions, with the legendary Mad Frankie Fraser.

Above: Even in his early twenties Bindon was an assured member of London's swinging party scene.

Top: Always in the spotlight, Bindon came alive in front of the camera. This was during a holiday in Malta with his great friend Alan Stanton (holding the camera).

Bottom: Pictured with teenage Miley Khailani, daughter of Bindon's schoolfriend Barry D'Arcy, whom he rescued from a number of potentially dangerous situations.

Above left: Beautiful model Mona Stanton enjoyed a close friendship with Bindon for many years.

Top right: Bindon's highly publicised encounter with Princess Margaret in Mustique led to a bizarre relationship.

Above right: Bindon's tempestuous relationship with posh debutant-turned-model Vicky Hodge lasted more than ten years.

Bindon's friend Dana Gillespie (pictured *bottom right*) took numerous snaps in Mustique. Some years later Bindon's girlfriend Vicky Hodge 'borrowed' the above missing photos of Bindon and Princess Margaret from their album and never returned them. Lionel Bart, the famous composer, is pictured top right.

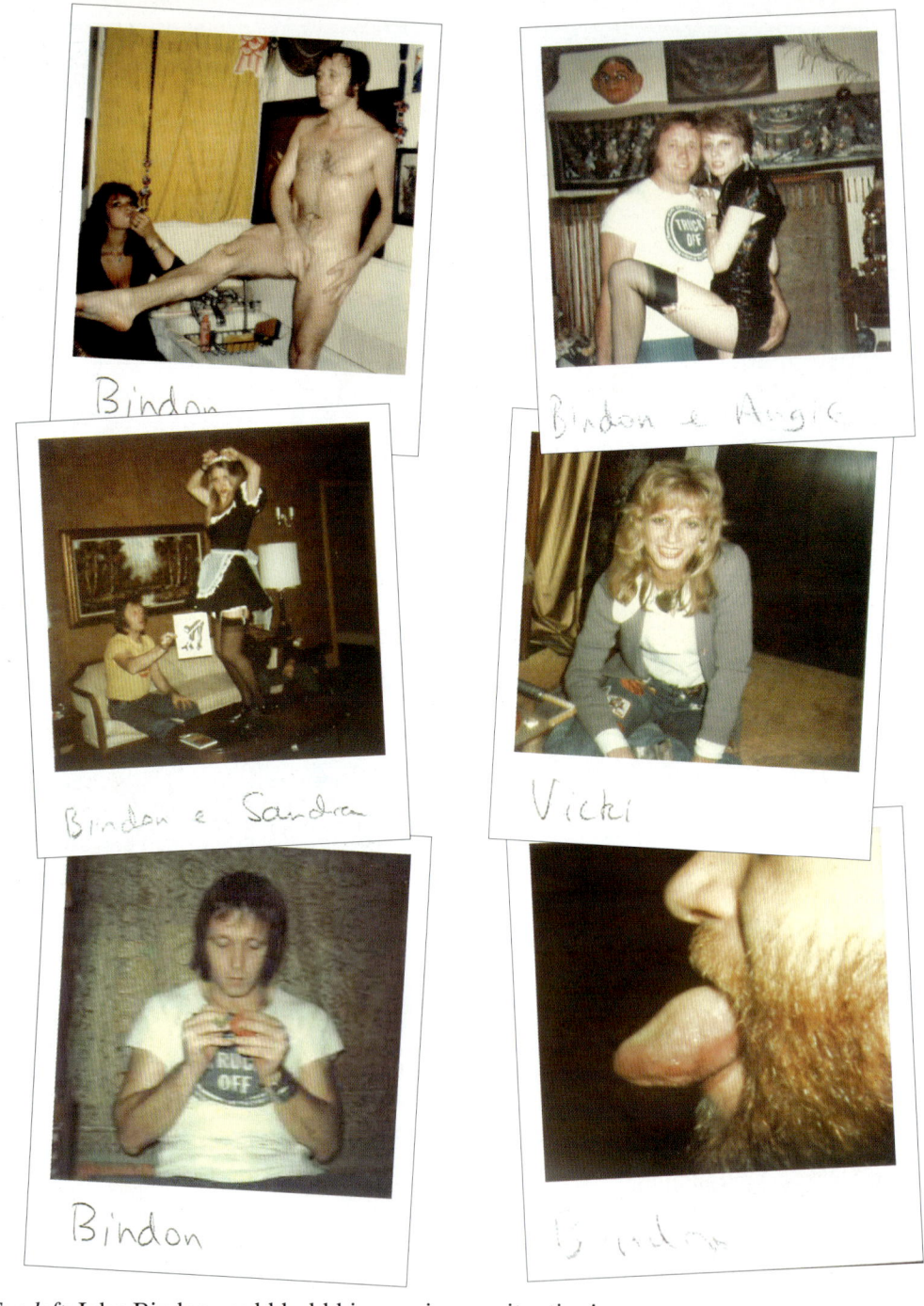

Top left: John Bindon could hold his own in any situation!

Top right: David Bowie's wife Angie couldn't resist Bindon's 'charms'.

Middle left: The 'Bindon effect' on women meant that many were like putty in his hands.

Middle right: Vicki hodge.

Above left: Bindon rolls up some 'puff', the only drug he regularly took.

Above right: The length of his tongue wasn't the only thing that women adored about Bindon!

Bindon

Me & Bindon

Bindon

Vicki & John

Bindon

Bindon loved to party, and also had a reputation for rescuing beautiful models from drug dens by throwing them over his shoulder! Naturally, neither Dana Gillespie, who kindly supplied all these photos, nor Vicki Hodge were among them!

Top: Bindon posing just near the spot where he bravely leaped into the River Thames to try and rescue a drowning man.

Bottom: The business card for Bindon's only ever straight job!

Chapter Nine

connections. 'We were told a family called the Hennessys had helped Bindon escape. After that I got word that he was definitely in the south.'

Meanwhile, Fleet Street was blissfully unaware that celebrity criminal turned actor John Bindon was at the top of the police wanted list. The first reports of a stabbing had John Darke playing centre stage. MAN STABBED TO DEATH AT CLUB was the headline of one of the early stories in the *Evening News*. The only giveaway paragraph read:

> Police said they thought the incident was a gang fight between rival factions, adding: 'The men involved were not youths. They were all middle-aged.' One local resident told the paper: 'I saw this man running around with blood all over his clothes. Then I saw the man lying on the ground. He obviously had serious wounds as there was blood pouring from his chest. It was dreadful.'

The *Evening News* then focused on Darke's colourful background:

> John Darke was well known in the Fulham area. In 1969 he was acquitted at the Old Bailey after being charged with several other men with an armed robbery at the BOAC terminal at Victoria in which more than £12,000 was stolen. Three of the men accused with him were found guilty and jailed for terms ranging from 12 to 14 years. Darke was sent to prison for seven months at the same time on a charge of handling a stolen driving licence.

The paper also stated that police were hunting for two men speeding away in a Land Rover-type vehicle which drove the wrong way down a one-way street near the Yacht Club. One occupant was described as tall, wearing jeans and a brown leather bomber jacket.

Bindon's beautiful blonde Swedish model lover Mona saw a report of the killing on the TV news the following day. 'I knew immediately the man with a brown leather jacket must have been John.. So I went to The Man in the Moon pub in the King's Road and spoke to John's friend Bobby Buckley and asked him if John was all right. I left my phone number and the following day Johnny Bindon telephoned. It was so sweet that he rang. He said he was all right and not to worry about him.'

Having been quizzed heavily by the police, Vicki Hodge took a break with friends for a few days. At her Fulham flat, a man called Bobby answered all press calls by announcing he was a friend of Bindon's and that they should call back in two weeks' time. Vicki had decided she wanted to get out of the heat for a while.

On 2 December 1978, George Mould decided to announce publicly that John Bindon was his number-one suspect. This revelation sparked a virtual avalanche of calls from villains in west London. 'Some were trying to say he was a hit man, which I did not believe for one second,' explained Mould. 'It just didn't fit, although I suppose it was possible. Some people on the streets were saying he'd done jobs for the Krays and the Richardsons but not necessarily for money, more for respect. So for the moment it was a possibility that I couldn't yet discount.'

One of the first newspapers to break the story of

Chapter Nine

Bindon's involvement in the murder was the *Sunday People* on 3 December 1978. They headlined their story POLICE HUNT KNIFED TV TOUGH GUY.

> Actor John Bindon, well-known film and TV tough guy, is being sought by police probing the death of a man in a club brawl. Bindon, long-time boyfriend of model Vicki Hodge and also a recent escort of former Bunny Girl Serena Williams, was himself badly injured. Bindon has vanished leaving behind a trail of blood. Police believe he has vital evidence which will help them. But they fear he may be too badly injured to come forward ... Detectives working from an incident room at Fulham Police Station have checked hospitals in an attempt to trace Bindon. The Ranelagh Yacht Club, hidden away in a back alley off Ranelagh Gardens under the arches of Putney Bridge station, has been closed indefinitely.

Other newspapers relished linking the name of such a well-known celebrity to a gangland murder. One article in the *Daily Express*, headlined MYSTERY OF TV TOUGH JOHN, reported that police had 'spoken to two of six-footer Bindon's girlfriends'. One police spokesman told the paper, 'They've been interviewed in the course of routine enquiries. We wanted to see if they could help us contact him. He has just vanished since the incident. Bindon's wounds were such that he must have required hospital attention.'

At St Vincent's Hospital in Dublin, Bindon had lost so much blood that he had had an emergency blood transfusion. His chest wound was still bleeding and he was coughing up blood. Surgeons also found that one of the stab wounds had even nicked his heart. By now, many in the underworld knew where Bindon was, and he feared some of them might be after him to exact some kind of revenge. He knew he wasn't safe, and was starting to wonder if he would be better off in the custody of the cops.

Back in London, George Mould's officers were finding that Chelsea and Fulham had gone very quiet. 'Everyone was trying to keep a lower profile because the bluebottles were coming out of every nook and cranny,' explained one of Bindon's oldest west-London pals. Over in south London, the Scotland Yard team who had targeted John Darke for months were delighted that he had been killed. Detective Terry Babbidge said, 'The man was a grass. It was a result when he turned up dead in the Yacht Club. John Darke was the type of man who would carry a knife in church. When he walked into a pub it emptied. People were terrified of him. Darke was a thoroughly nasty man and Bindon did us all a favour.'

George Mould was still tearing his hair out trying to discover where Bindon was hiding; then he got a phone call at Hammersmith Police Station. 'One of my team came into my office and said, "You've had a phone call from Dublin, fella called John asked to speak to George." I had never talked to Bindon in my life. It was just "John from Dublin", nothing more.'

Minutes later, Mould got another phone call. This time it was put through to his office. 'George?' Bindon's voice hesitated. 'George? It's John Bindon.'

'Hello, John. Where are you?'

Chapter Nine

'I'm in hospital. I want to talk to you, George. Can you come and see me?'

'Where are you?'

'I'm at St Vincent's. I gotta talk to you.'

'Good.'

'That Darky, George, he was a fuckin' animal.'

'Don't go away now, John.'

'I can't. I got Old Bill all around the place.'

In fact, the Irish police, the Guarda, had just turned up at the hospital to investigate the identity of the mystery man with the serious stab wounds. A few minutes later Mould got a call from the Irish police saying, 'I've got a man here who says he's …'

'Turned out they'd surrounded the hospital,' recalled Mould. 'I went over by plane next day and was met by a DI from the Guarda, but the British police were not too popular over there at the time because of all the problems with the IRA.' In fact, John Bindon didn't like or trust his Dublin police guards. He was extremely worried they might grass him up to one of the villains who were after him.

Mould's first meeting with Bindon was a disaster because Bindon had a locally hired lawyer present advising him not to answer any questions. 'Bindon kept saying that he wanted to talk to me, but this lawyer was adamant so we were getting nowhere,' recalled Mould. 'The room had three beds in it, but he was the only one in there and I noticed a fire escape by the window. There were tubes coming out of every part of him. He was a very sick man, unable to move, but he seemed desperate to talk, or rather act out what had happened.'

Mould was told he'd have to wait for another lawyer to

arrive from London, so he made an appointment to see Bindon again at three o'clock that afternoon. He winked at Bindon, and Bindon winked back, leading Mould to believe that he wanted to co-operate if they could snatch some private time together. 'I went back to see Bindon at two instead of three, after getting in to see him via the fire escape. He was on his own and he knew what I was up to. The Guarda were outside the room and had no idea I'd slipped in to see Bindon. Bindon skated over the actual fight, but for a man who was so ill he acted superbly. He was a likeable fella in many ways. I was his best friend immediately. He told me, "People in that club all had knives. That Bohm bloke was a right nutter." Bindon said Bohm had carried two blades down each trouser leg. He eventually admitted his own role, but I had to decide whether it was murder or self-defence. He obviously enjoyed having me as his audience. He said it was a fight and others were involved and that he'd been picked on.'

Then Bindon astonished Mould by mentioning his friendship with Princess Margaret out of the blue. 'George,' he said. 'I'm worried all this business could land her in the shit. There's nothing in it. There really is nothing in it. Make sure the powers that be know that I'm keeping my lips sealed, won't you?'

Mould wondered why Bindon was so obsessed with mentioning Princess Margaret. 'I'll do what I can, John,' he promised.

Bindon then changed the subject to boast about his successful escape to Ireland. 'Bindon said all the reporters were chasing after Vicki and everyone else, but those Catholic hospitals like St Vincent's are very tight and the

Chapter Nine

press never got a sniff of it. The nuns had the final word on everything.'

Mould spent a total of forty-five minutes with Bindon. Then, as the Guarda officer appeared in the doorway with the new lawyer from London, he turned to him and said, 'John, the extradition is going to take ages.'

'But I want to come back,' said Bindon.

'Well, we'll fix it for you then.'

'I don't think Bindon liked being shut up in that hospital in Ireland,' Mould later explained, 'and he knew he'd have to come back eventually. But the Irish police were not keen, especially because I'd seen him on my own.'

Mould was escorted from Bindon's hospital bedside by furious Guarda officers. 'I flew back to London knowing Bindon had to volunteer to return to the UK. His lawyers didn't want him to come back. In London, I got more phone calls from him saying he wanted to come back but his brief was saying he shouldn't. So I said, "If you come back, I'll have you met and brought to Fulham nick." He said, "Am I going to be charged?" I said, "You probably are. When I talk to you in Fulham nick we'll decide. You'll be locked up, so don't think that you're going to walk because you're not."'

'Fair enough, George. I know you have a job to do,' replied a very calm Bindon.

George Mould was now pretty confident he had his man in the bag.

In the middle of all these negotiations, Serena Williams turned up at Bindon's hospital bedside. He had been planning a romantic weekend in Dublin before going back to London. He even called Vicki Hodge to explain the

'Serena situation'. 'Now listen, Hodgy, Serena's over here.' Vicki had been betrayed as usual, especially since she had once again put herself completely on the line for him. She had risked everything for him, and now he was flaunting that woman in front of her again. She said she would never forgive Bindon, but few believed her. When asked how she felt by one friend, she replied, 'All I hope is that he's safe.'

There were rumours in London that, once Fulham Police had caught up with Bindon in St Vincent's Hospital, they struck an extraordinary deal allowing him to come back to London at his own leisure. In return he was believed to have provided vital information about the murder of John Darke. One of Bindon's oldest friends later explained, 'What the police did was completely out of order. They implied that Bindon had grassed up other villains in order to get himself an easy ticket back to London. It was complete bollocks! All it did was ensure that Bindon now had a price on his head.'

Scotland Yard requested reinforced security from their Irish counterparts after claiming new information about threats to Bindon had been received. He was reported still to be physically weak. One Dublin police officer told reporters, 'If he had left things much longer he would have been in no danger – he would have been dead. He must have the constitution of a carthorse.'

Back in London, gangsters were insisting to anyone who would listen that there were *no* plans to rub out Bindon, and that many of the stories had been deliberately spread to help the acting career of the publicity-hungry hard man. One source close to the Darke family said, 'It's bollocks to say there's a contract out on Bindon's life.' One newspaper

Chapter Nine

even managed to track down John Darke's mother Irene who said, 'My son was taken to his death but we don't know why. John [Darke] was a villain. He mixed with some rough characters and did some bad things – but everybody loved him.' But Bindon was now a wanted man with more publicity than he could ever get when he was an actor.

By 7 December, his health seemed to be improving and newspapers were reporting that he was expected to fly back to Britain under armed guard within the next three days. Officially, police refused to discuss the movements because they still feared gang bosses had put a price on his head. The following day, Bindon rang Mould yet again. 'Right, I'm coming back on the ferry train into London tomorrow.'

Mould told him that was fine on condition he agreed to speak to the police without his brief being present.

'Fine,' he replied.

Bindon might have been out of danger in terms of his injuries, but police still had the headache of keeping him alive. A team of detectives from Fulham were assembled to get him back to London safely. On 8 December, he was escorted out of St Vincent's Hospital into a waiting car that secretly left through a side entrance; but his supposedly secret journey back to London eventually turned into a complete farce when newspapers managed to snatch photos of him with his police escort at Holyhead on the night ferry. With his head covered by a rug, he was hurried from the ship by his CID escort using a separate exit that kept them well away from other passengers, and customs checks were waived. He was then driven to the station to catch a train to Bangor, where he boarded an express for London's Euston station. He was also accompanied by his solicitor.

Bindon and his police escorts paid excess fares of £31 to move him into a first-class compartment where all the blinds were immediately drawn to keep out prying press men. However, the only nearby passengers were a *Daily Star* reporter and photographer, who immediately snatched a number of shots of Bindon and his police minders. As the train approached Euston it was switched at the last minute from platform thirteen to platform one, where two unmarked police cars waited. Bindon, who had grown a beard during his stay in hospital, was almost unrecognisable as he was whisked away in one of the waiting vehicles.

On arrival at Fulham Police Station that Thursday, 9 December, Bindon surrendered his personal items to the station sergeant and then allowed a police doctor to examine him. George Mould recalled, 'First the doctor looked at him and asked Bindon if he was prepared to talk to me, and he said fine, so we started the interview almost immediately. I always kept a doctor there to keep an eye on his injuries and because they make the perfect witness. I didn't want any claims of beatings or whatever. Bindon and I eventually had a good long talk. He gave me a fuller picture of what happened that night. He admitted carrying a knife and ruled everyone including Vicki Hodge out of involvement, but I knew he was acting the whole time. Then his mouthpiece lawyer turned up, although at least he didn't know what Bindon had already said.'

Tape recorders for interviews were not mandatory in those days, so Mould took notes during and after the

Chapter Nine

meeting. 'But these were just for guidance, not to be used in actual evidence.'

One of Mould's strongest memories of talking to Bindon on that first day at Fulham nick was his pride about the Thames rescue attempt more than ten years earlier. 'It was all part of his act, I suppose. He said to me, "I got a fuckin' medal, George."' He also cracked a few jokes. 'They were all stories relating to him and his sexual prowess, but it broke the ice between us so I didn't care. He'd virtually given himself up. He was in an untenable situation. He had no option. I had my man and I was happy.'

Minutes after that first proper interview ended, Vicki Hodge grabbed yet more newspaper headlines by tottering into Fulham Police Station on her six-inch heels with some hot food for her jailed lover. Thirty minutes later, an unmarked car with Vicki in the passenger seat screeched out of the station. 'It was the first time I'd met her,' recalled George. 'She was always wearing very short, skimpy clothing that was not really suitable for the time of year. She pretended to be helpful, but wasn't really. She never explained her role in his escape because she would have been charged. I found the smile on her face particularly annoying as it seemed to be there for the cameras at all times. She didn't like me at all. She continually suggested that Bindon had been put upon all his life and he was hard done by. I don't like Vicki Hodge. She is flirty and the younger officers loved having her in the station. She was photographed as she entered and left the station. She loved the drama of having her picture taken.'

Within days of Bindon's arrest, *Daily Mail* gossip columnist Nigel Dempster circulated a note to warn other journalists on the paper that Princess Margaret had never even met Bindon. It read, 'Could a note please be made concerning references to Princess Margaret and John Bindon, to the effect that not only is she not an acquaintance but she has never danced with him and has never been introduced to him.' Dempster insisted rumours of a 'friendship' between Bindon and Margaret were rubbish, and references to the trip to the West Indies were removed from many newspaper libraries so that the stories would not be repeated during the countdown to Bindon's trial. In fact, Kensington Palace feared that the blaze of publicity surrounding Bindon's arrest for murder might spark further investigations into those earlier rumours about a romance between Bindon and 'PM', so the princess herself contacted Dempster to ask him to publish the strongest possible denials.

Bindon's return home to face the music sparked an extraordinary showing of loyalty from Vicki Hodge, despite their bust-up over Serena Williams. Day after day she visited him in custody. Bindon was facing a murder charge and Vicki was reduced to drawing the dole. Their life had turned upside down, but she was determined not to abandon him in his hour of need.

Chapter Ten

The day after Bindon's return to London – 10 December 1978 – he was officially charged with murdering John Darke. 'Then I had the chore of continuing to gather in evidence to decide if he really was the man who did it,' explained DCS George Mould. On Monday, 13 December 1978, Bindon – slumped and still in pain – made his first court appearance in the dock at Horseferry Road Magistrates' Court. Dressed in his customary leather jacket and faded jeans, he coughed occasionally during the hearing and was clearly in great discomfort. His defence counsel Anthony Block asked DCS Mould, 'From the evidence gathered together, does it appear that the wounds were inflicted on Mr Bindon before the wounds inflicted on the deceased man?'

'That would seem possible,' replied Mould, who then revealed to the court that Bindon had contacted him from

Ireland and said he wanted to return to the UK once he had sufficiently recovered from his wounds. Vicki sat in the dock of the public gallery as Bindon was remanded in custody for a week and ordered to be kept in the hospital wing at Brixton Prison. He looked bitterly disappointed not to get bail.

Meanwhile, Vicki – looking radiant in one of her favourite ultra-short mini-skirts – told the waiting press she was planning for Bindon's Christmas celebrations: 'I am not allowed into prison on Christmas Day, so my Christmas will not start until Boxing Day when I can see him.' Sure enough, on Boxing Day Vicki made sure she was photographed looking as glamorous as ever in black leather thigh-high boots and a fur coat when she arrived to see Bindon at Brixton. After giving him a bag of fruit and sweets and enjoying a fifteen-minute visit, she left sadly, gripping the arm of a close friend. She told reporters, 'John is still sick but is being treated well. I was able to hold his hands and transmit my love to him. I know he is innocent.'

A few days later she told a gossip columnist on the *Daily Express* that her appearances at the jail were 'morale boosters' for Bindon. 'My New Year resolution is to see this thing resolved one way or another.'

By 5 January, Vicki was telling reporters that Bindon was definitely on the mend from his injuries. 'They have been very good to him in jail and are doing everything they can,' she said. 'He's not 100 per cent, but he is all right. Everybody is delighted that he's getting better.' Vicki was speaking outside Horseferry Road Magistrates' Court where Bindon had been remanded in custody to Brixton Prison hospital once again.

Chapter Ten

Not long after Bindon's arrest, George Mould received a visit from the very same MI5 spooks who visited Bindon shortly after his second trip to Mustique. Mould told this author, 'All this Margaret stuff kept coming up and then people from our side came to see me and said, "We don't want this coming out." I told them, "Look, it's nothing to do with my inquiry."'

Mould believes to this day there was a 'gross overreaction' by MI5 at the time of Bindon's arrest. 'Look, Bindon was pulled in by the security services and that was it, and to be fair to John Bindon he didn't talk about it, so what more could anyone do about it?'

On 12 January, Bindon appeared before magistrates at Horseferry Road once more in a new bid to get bail. Vicki sat avidly listening to the proceedings as Detective Superintendent Michael Huines, opposing bail, told the court, 'I feel that further offences may be committed while he is on bail.' The police chief was then asked what those offences might be. 'He might be placed in a position which could lead to an offence such as the one already committed.'

Magistrate Edmond McDermott asked, 'Another murder?'

'It is possible, yes.'

Bail was refused and Bindon was sent back to Brixton. He later said he was outraged that they could imply he might murder someone else. He had already insisted to George Mould that John Darke had stabbed him first and he only used his knife in self-defence, which was why he intended to plead not guilty. Mould, however, made it clear to Bindon that he would pursue the murder charge all the way to the Old Bailey.

Meanwhile, in a letter to Vicki, Bindon wrote from prison, 'Dear Hodgy, eleven years with you is the best sentence I ever had. I miss you so much. That's all part of loving you.'

Vicki later admitted she had smuggled tranquillisers into Brixton because she was so worried about his mental health. 'I used to take him a Mandrax wrapped in cling film, which I put in my mouth and then gave to him through a big kiss. That would keep him cool for the whole day. It was nice for him. I didn't want him to explode like a keg of dynamite in Brixton Prison. He wouldn't have survived it.' Vicki proudly dressed extra provocatively during those jail visits, and later admitted, 'I used to wear really tight trousers, short skirts and long boots. If all of the other prisoners whistled at me, it was a good day.'

On 20 February, Bindon's committal proceedings to decide if there was enough evidence to try him for murder hit the front pages after prosecutors implied he was a contract killer hired specifically to murder John Darke. The *Daily Mail* headline the following morning said it all: ACTOR 'WAS PAID FOR CONTRACT TO KILL GANG RIVAL'. Prosecuting counsel David Boyd told Lambeth Magistrates' Court that Bindon went to the Yacht Club 'with murder in his heart'. 'Bindon went to the club to kill Darke, having been paid a sum of money by a third party as a contract to kill.' The allegations were fiercely denied by Bindon's defence team.

Sitting alongside co-defendants – Darke's friends Begbe, Bohm and Galbraith – Bindon barely moved a muscle as the court heard gruesome details about the actual killing. They were told that Darke kneeled astride Bindon, and

Chapter Ten

stabbed him repeatedly before getting up and standing back. Boyd told the court, 'Despite his serious injuries, Bindon managed to get up and fatally stab Darke repeatedly. He also stabbed Begbe, severing his nose. Darke was carried out and died within minutes.'

The court was then told Bindon's response after he was questioned by George Mould in that Dublin hospital: 'I thought he had done me. I got the knife into him two or three times.' Anthony Block, defending Bindon, protested at the suggestion that the actor was some kind of contract killer. 'There was not a trace of such an allegation in any of the papers the prosecution served,' he said.

Also giving evidence that afternoon at court was Roy Dennis. He said he had first been attacked by Darke and then saw Bindon approach. 'He put his arms around Darke or got hold of him. Bindon saved my life – I think I would have got stabbed again and again by Darke.'

In court the following day, the damaging hit-man allegations were made by Bindon's fellow Brixton inmate David Murphy. Murphy claimed that Bindon had told him in their cell he had been offered £10,000 to kill Darke. The court heard that the contract had been taken out because Darke had been paid money to burn down a nightclub but still wanted more and was trying to blackmail people. Murphy told magistrates he and Bindon played Scrabble together in their cell and Bindon even joked about Darke in front of him by looking down at the floor and muttering, 'Is it warm enough for you down there, Darkie? Is it hot enough?'

On 21 February, a statement by Bindon was read out in court. 'I remember Darke kneeling beside me trying to stab me through the heart. I tried to stop him and he tried to stab me in the eye. He cut me on the face. Lenny Osborne grabbed the knife and saved my life.'

Bindon's counsel Anthony Block reiterated to the court there was no hard evidence to suggest Bindon had been hired to kill Darke. 'There has never been a hint at previous hearings of these allegations.' Two days later, Flying Squad Detective Sergeant John Ross told the court that he had paid Darke in the region of £1,000 over the previous two and a half years. Ross said his superiors had authorised the payments, most of which were for information leading to the arrest in October 1977 of two men on armed robbery charges.

Next came a statement from Darke's friend Ernie Begbe that claimed two men were 'doing' Darke with a knife in the Yacht Club. 'I saw the two of them doing John [Darke] and I went up behind them to pull them off. They both had knives and were leaning over him stabbing him.'

Bindon's friend and fellow actor Billy Murray called Bindon's mum Ciss to see how he was coping, and she begged him to go and visit her son in Brixton prison. 'He looked gaunt and had lost loads of weight,' Murray recalled, 'and wasn't confident about getting off the charges. He wasn't having a bad time inside because he was tough, but he hated being locked up twenty-three hours a day.'

On 13 March 1979, Bindon was committed to stand for trial for the murder of John Darke. A convicted south-London armed robber, who had already been accused of hiring him to kill Darke, stood up in the court and described the charges against him as a 'fabricated charade' set up to throw a smokescreen around robbery charges he

Chapter Ten

himself faced. The man insisted he had only heard of the hit-man allegations through newspapers and Bindon's lawyer Mr Block.

Block said there was no case to answer against Bindon, but magistrate Edmund McDermott told the court, 'These are matters a jury should decide.' Bindon was sent for trial. Afterwards the ever-present Vicki Hodge gushed to reporters, 'I am heartbroken at this result. But I'm going to stand by him. He has done nothing wrong.'

Three crucial witnesses went missing in the run-up to Bindon's trial: one of the robbers grassed up by Darke to police before his death, Lennie Osborne and Ernest Begbe. Osborne and Begbe had both jumped bail. Then, a leading south-London solicitor who acted for one of the missing men was twice threatened with death if he didn't drop his involvement in the case. He later told a reporter, 'It really is rather like the old-time Chicago gangland era. Two different men have burst into my office quite prepared to kill me.'

A few weeks later – in April 1979 – Bindon was told that one of his rare recent TV roles, in the series *Hazell*, had been shelved until after his murder trial because TV chiefs feared the episode could influence the jury. In the programme, Bindon played a well-dressed gunman who killed another mobster. The TV company explained, 'On the advice of our lawyers the episode will not be transmitted on the date planned. Attention is drawn to Mr Bindon's trial.'

Vicki said Bindon was disappointed. 'It was a realistic part,' she told reporters. 'But John favoured showing it as soon as possible. If people have not got the intelligence to differentiate between fact and fiction, they should not be serving on a jury.'

Vicki also had other things on her mind, including a promise to marry Bindon as soon as he was released from prison. 'I see John every day and now that the dust has settled a bit, he looks much better and much fitter,' she explained, before making sure she informed reporters that she was in the middle of writing her life story. 'John takes up a great part of the book, but it's difficult concentrating at the moment.'

A few weeks later, the body of John Darke was finally laid to rest in a cemetery in south-east London. Police watched from a discreet distance as more than a hundred family and friends turned up for the ceremony.

Vicki took Joey Pyle for a visit to see Bindon in Brixton. He wanted Pyle to tell their old friend Lennie Osborne that he wasn't upset about rumours that Osborne had turned police grass since jumping bail. Oddly, a couple of months later Pyle was charged with conspiracy to pervert the course of justice during police investigations into John Darke's murder. Pyle was detained at his home in Morden, south London, during a massive series of police raids on homes all over the city.

On 20 August, Bindon slashed his arm in protest at being transferred out of Brixton Prison's remand wing to the austere surroundings of nearby Wandsworth. The thirty-four-year-old actor needed six stitches in a wound he had made with a tin-can top. He was eventually taken by ambulance to the hospital wing at Wandsworth. Vicki explained, 'As soon as John cut himself, rumours went round the prison that he'd tried to kill himself. He told me afterwards that the stories were rubbish. I was shocked

Chapter Ten

when I visited him on Friday. He looked very tired. He was under drugs and was like a zombie. He could hardly talk to me. Nobody realises the strain he has been under, being in prison for eight months.'

Greg Hodal went to visit him in Wandsworth to try and boost his morale. He also wanted to see his pal because his incarceration meant Bindon was going to miss his wedding in London. Hodal and another friend decided to lighten proceedings by turning up at Wandsworth in top hats and tails. 'It was hilarious. Three guards brought John in to see us and they were all laughing hysterically because not many folk turn up to jail dressed for a wedding.' Hodal said Bindon seemed in reasonable spirits, although he was far from confident about the outcome of his trial.

In September, Vicki claimed in the *Daily Mirror* that more threats had been made against Bindon's life while he was on remand. She also claimed that pirate copies of photos of Bindon with Princess Margaret in Mustique were circulating, to which she had no connection, and she insisted her own set of private snaps was not for sale. She even told the *Mirror*, 'This person – whoever it is – just wants to cause embarrassment by selling those carefree pictures for base commercial profit. I think it would be in very poor taste for somebody to try and sell them.'

Vicki insisted she had no plans to flog her own holiday snaps of Bindon with Princess Margaret, even though they were worth tens of thousands of pounds on the tabloid-newspaper market. 'We have our own photographs, but I'm not going round showing the snaps to anyone. They're part of our private collection. I wouldn't dream of selling them to pay for anything,' she said.

One newspaper published yet another thinly disguised denial from the princess via one of her friends: 'As soon as he arrived on the island, my detective recognised him and made sure there was no possibility of an embarrassing situation. Yet there have been reports of my dancing with the man!' The carefully orchestrated campaign by Margaret's friends to deny any connection to Bindon had continued since the Nigel Dempster story just after Bindon's arrest. As one close friend of the princess's explained many years later, 'It was imperative that Margaret continued to distance herself from him.'

Meanwhile the ever-loyal Vicki even brought Bindon's other girlfriends to visit him in prison. She also visited many of his west-London friends collecting for the 'Darke Fund' to help pay for his defence costs. She confessed that sometimes she turned up at jail to see Bindon without wearing any knickers. 'That was typical Vicki. She was besotted by John and would do anything to hold on to him,' explained one of Bindon's oldest pals.

The story of an actor whose real-life activities led to murder was about to unfold in Number One Court at the Old Bailey, the most famous criminal stage in the world. Bindon's future now relied on him giving the finest performance of his life.

Chapter Eleven

On 23 October 1979, John Bindon pleaded not guilty to murdering John Darke. Bindon, whose address was given as his parents' flat at Sullivan Court, was also charged with causing an affray at the club along with Darke's associates Raymond Bohm and George Galbraith. They all denied the charges.

The jury heard how Bindon lay spread-eagled on the floor of the Yacht Club pleading for his life in the middle of his fight with Darke. The court was also told that, despite severe wounds, Bindon fought back and stabbed his attacker to death with his then girlfriend Serena Williams's hunting knife. Prosecuting counsel Allan Green informed the court that it would be alleged Bindon had been hired on a £20,000 contract to kill Darke, a police informant. There would even be a claim that Bindon confessed all to a fellow prisoner while he awaited trial in

Brixton. But Green admitted to the jury that two key witnesses — Bindon's friend Lennie Osborne and Darke associate Ernie Begbe — were still on the missing list.

The court then heard that, in the hospital in Dublin, Bindon claimed to police that he had been threatened with death shortly before that fateful evening in the Yacht Club, but he had stressed that no one involved in the knife fight was part of that same 'problem'. Johnny Gillette then told the court that the fight in the Yacht Club was 'a nightmare'. 'Bindon was defending himself. It was horrifying. There was my friend, perhaps my closest friend, being stabbed and covered in blood.' He also informed the court that Bindon was a popular and amusing man and that a lot of people were jealous of his personality.

Describing how he saw Roy Dennis being stabbed, Gillette said that Bindon had gone over to intervene and in the affray fell to the ground. 'He was trapped between a table and the jukebox. Then some other gentlemen came along, three of them surrounded him and one was on top of him. The man sitting on top of him was stabbing him. I just stood there, looking at my pal being stabbed. I was horrified. I thought he was dead and I was looking for the best way to get out of the club. I just ran for my life.'

Then up stepped Alan Stanton — although no one at the Old Bailey that day realised how close he was to Bindon. The prosecution had originally called him to describe Bindon's attack on Darke but, donning serious-looking spectacles, he cleverly turned around the prosecution questions and ended up telling the court how Bindon was the victim of an unprovoked attack. As one of Stanton's oldest friends later told this author, 'Alan was fuckin'

Chapter Eleven

brilliant. He looked more like the mad professor than a blagger with a record as long as your arm. It was all planned between Alan and John during visits to prison before the trial, and it worked like a dream because Alan ended up giving evidence that showed John hadn't started all the aggro.'

Then the Old Bailey heard from Bindon's fellow Brixton inmate David Murphy, who now also insisted that, besides being contracted to kill Darke, Bindon had also confessed to killing a second man with a shotgun hidden in a bunch of flowers. Murphy described how Bindon carried out his earlier hit, even referring to the moment he knocked on his victim's door and said, 'I've got a present for you from a friend.' Then, said Murphy, 'Bindon let him have it.'

Murphy, himself a convicted murderer, also claimed Bindon had provided the name of his paymaster for the alleged Darke contract killing: It was a man whom he claimed was a part-owner of the Yacht Club. 'He said there were a couple of reasons for him being killed. He said Darke had been on a couple of murder charges the previous year and had walked out of the magistrates' court. He added he was either very, very lucky or he knew he was a grass. He said that Darke was paid to burn down a nightclub that he didn't actually do himself, but he paid others to do it. It was one of those ventures where you either make lots of money or you don't, but it didn't, so they went after the insurance money. Darke wasn't satisfied with the money he was paid for burning the club down and said he'd put a black on others to get more money.'

Murphy admitted to the Old Bailey jury he had many criminal convictions going back to 1968 and said the reason he was now volunteering evidence was because he didn't agree with violence unless it was in self-defence. 'Bindon did not say how the contract to kill was to be done,' he added. 'He said the row in the club seemed to be a good enough excuse to get in and do it. He said he'd discussed the facts with a guy called Lennie Osborne. He said he went over and approached Darke and stabbed him. He said Darke had got him on the floor and tried to stab him in the eye, but he turned and he stabbed him in the side of the head instead.'

Murphy also told the court that Bindon had explained how he fled to Ireland. 'He said he went there with Lennie Osborne, but they split up and that Lennie had IRA connections and they looked after him.' As Murphy finished off his evidence, John Bindon rolled his eyes and grimaced.

On 25 October, Joey Pyle was cleared at Marlborough Street Court of conspiring to pervert the course of justice concerning the death of Johnny Darke. He was bailed for £5,000 because he still faced two charges of plotting to handle stolen American Express travellers' cheques, possessing forged passports and handling eleven tins of stolen paint. Back at the Old Bailey, on 29 October it was Bindon's turn to take the stand. To start with, he admitted all his earlier convictions. Then he told the court about alleged death threats from a 'Mr X' whose name he wrote down on a piece of paper. The judge, jury and counsel for the defence and prosecution were allowed to see the name. He claimed Mr X had threatened him a number of times after he began his relationship with Vicki Hodge nearly ten years earlier. He said he had refused to go to the police because of his own 'murky' past.

Chapter Eleven

Bindon told the jury he feared Mr X might take reprisals against his family. 'I don't want to name this man,' Bindon told Mr Justice Mars-Jones. 'I believe that if I talked about him I would have reason to be very concerned about the safety of my brother and sister, and they have nothing to do with this.' The mystery man was described by Bindon as a 'lunatic' when he had been drinking. 'It was obvious to me what sway he held with others.' The prosecution weren't impressed by the claims, but Bindon wasn't finished yet. The jury heard how he had turned his back on a life of crime after meeting Vicki Hodge, although that had of course resulted in these mystery threats from Mr X. 'On the one hand I was a working actor, but on the other hand my murky past had caught up with me. That's why I never reacted as any law-abiding citizen would have reacted and should do.'

Talking about the lead-up to the killing of John Darke, Bindon said he had accepted the gift of a hunting knife from Serena Williams because he had taken the threats by Mr X seriously. 'I thought that if the man caught me with a few of his friends and without any witnesses I could be very seriously injured or wind up dead.' He also said he thought at the time that the attack at the Yacht Club was the result of these threats, but he now realised this was not the case.

Bindon's delivery of his evidence about the actual fight was every bit as dramatic as any acting role he had ever performed. 'I thought I was going to die,' he said breathlessly. 'I felt the knife go in. There was a pain and a great coldness. It was like an icicle stuck there.' He described the night of John Darke's killing as being 'almost like a ballet. Darke was just sort of prodding Roy Dennis with the knife. Dennis was shouting for help but no one went to his aid. I thought Dennis had no defence and Darke wasn't going to stop. I felt sick because there I was, expecting trouble, and watching it happen to someone else. I waited for a second, then Darke went for him again round the head. Dennis gave a very high-pitched shriek like a trapped animal. I crossed the floor and grabbed Darke round the neck with my left arm. He made no attempt to get out of my grip and we stood immobile for a while. Then I felt a sharp blow to my back near my kidneys. I looked down and could see the knife under my right arm.'

Bindon said he then let go and moved away. As Darke lunged at him again he fell to the floor. After sipping from a glass of water, he went on to explain to the hushed courtroom, 'Darke sat astride me with the knife. To him it seemed fine and that was the proper place he should be. He was quite calm.'

But, said Bindon, that was when Darke knifed him again. 'I felt weak and my head was spinning. Blood was pouring out of my chest and eye. Darke was standing a few feet away with the knife still in his hand. He was saying something like, "I'll cut your head off." He then came towards me again and swung his arm with the knife in it. I thought I was going to die. I held my arm out with my knife in it. I was trying to keep him off me. But I can't recall feeling resistance to my knife. But I was expecting to drop down any minute. The next thing that happened people began separating us. Darke did not try to struggle out of my grip. Then I felt a sharp blow to my back. I looked

Chapter Eleven

down and saw a knife blade pointing under my left arm. This caused me to let go of Darke and back away.

'Darke pivoted round to face me. I dodged out of the way of the knife. He grabbed me by the arm, still holding the knife in his right hand. I smashed to the floor on my back by the jukebox. Darke got on top of me with his knee on my chest. He was saying, "You're going to go now." Then he stabbed me in the chest. I felt the blade going in and my body froze. I could see the handle of the knife sticking out of my chest. He took the knife out. I was literally begging him to stop. But he just gave me a bland smile. Then he started circling the blade round my face and talking to me in a quiet, soothing way. He was mesmerising me. Then he quickly jabbed it towards my left eye. I moved my head to the right and the blade went in the side of my head. At first I thought it had gone into my eye. At that moment I felt great fear more than pain. Again I shouted, "You are killing me, you are killing me," and I called for help.'

That, according to Bindon's testimony, was when Darke was grabbed from behind as he tried to cut Bindon's throat. Bindon grappled with him – it was a trial of strength. 'I could feel the point of the knife sticking into my neck, and he was trying to push it in further. Then he was pulled off me by somebody.'

Bindon told the hushed courtroom he felt he was dying. He looked straight into the eye of every member of the jury as he explained how blood was coming from his chest and head and running into his eyes. He vaguely remembered then getting to his feet. The sheath knife had almost come out of his boot during the struggle. 'I took the knife out of its sheath. Darke was standing two and a half paces away in a crouching posture, and I struck out at him.'

He said he remembered people separating them, then he was carried to a car where he lost consciousness. When he got out of the car, Vicki Hodge was there.

Suddenly, in the middle of all this dramatic evidence, John Bindon collapsed in the witness box after suffering what was later described as 'a severe asthmatic attack'. He was treated on the spot by medical staff and the judge adjourned the case.

Bindon always looked straight at the jury while giving evidence, but he later admitted he was bothered when some of them wouldn't look back at him. George Mould hailed Bindon's testimony as a 'masterful performance' worthy of an Oscar. And, despite rumours to the contrary, Mould remains convinced to this day that there were no actual attempts to tamper with the jury during the trial. 'We asked around and every member of the jury was told to call us if anything untoward happened, but, as far as the witnesses were concerned, you couldn't really give any of them protection because most of them were criminals.'

On 31 October, Bindon returned to explaining more about his murky past and the women in his life. Talking in a quiet, murmuring voice, he also continued strongly to deny ever accepting a £10,000 contract to murder John Darke. After his detailed and exhaustive testimony, Mr Justice Mars-Jones adjourned the trial early – and ordered a tired-looking Bindon to have another medical before he resumed the next day. 'I would like him to be examined before continuing so that I can be sure he is able to do himself justice.'

Chapter Eleven

On 1 November, Bindon broke down and cried while being asked why he hadn't told police about his knife attack on Darke. Bindon told the court he couldn't continue with his story because the memory of his wounds had upset him so much. 'It was akin to a woman being raped ... when you get someone on top of you and you have to do what they say.'

Then prosecutor Allan Green interrupted, 'The Crown suggests that, after the serious injuries you got from Darke, you got to your feet, got a knife out, crossed the length of that room and stabbed Darke to death. Is there any truth in that?'

'Not to my knowledge.'

The following day, the defence revealed the ace up their sleeve. Bindon was a friend to the stars, and the stars weren't afraid to help him out in his hour of need. Years ago, he had become friendly with Hollywood star Bob Hoskins; now Hoskins was called as a character witness. The prosecution immediately asked Hoskins why Bindon sometimes used the nickname Biffo, in the hope it would prove his propensity for violence. It backfired in spectacular fashion when Hoskins cheerily told the court, 'It's 'cos he's like a big, gentle bear. I mean he's so lovely and cuddly. Look at him.'

The court erupted in laughter, but the judge was not amused. 'I don't think we want any of your show-business behaviour here,' he told the actor.

George Mould was infuriated by Hoskins's evidence. 'Bob Hoskins's attitude was frivolous. The judge pulled him up on it by saying, 'This is a court room, not a theatre.' Bob Hoskins turned the case against us because he got the jury laughing. Everything seemed to go downhill from then on. The jury was star-struck by Hoskins. They were impressed. He was smiling across at Bindon and it did make a difference.'

On 5 November, prosecutor Allan Green began his summing-up to the jury by claiming Bindon was a natural liar and had been lying in particular about statements he had made to police. 'It isn't a case of the police putting words into his mouth. He is lying his head off.' The prosecutor also stated there was little dispute that Bindon had killed Darke. The question was whether he had intended to do so. He also pointed out that Bindon had known enough about what he was doing to remember Darke's last words.

The jury was then told that if they thought Bindon deliberately killed Darke during his counter-attack for revenge, after losing self-control, then they should at least find him guilty of manslaughter on the grounds of provocation. Bindon had earlier said from the witness box he was feeling neither angry nor humiliated at the time. But Green also reminded the jury of the pathologist's evidence that the stab wounds to Darke were struck with considerable force. 'He must have known that he was stabbing this man with a sharp knife, and must have intended at the least to do him serious physical injury. But was he acting in self-defence?' Green also claimed that all the defendants were put in one cell after their arrest, where they had shaken hands and agreed to let bygones by bygones, implying that they would all try and help each other to be found not guilty.

Then it was the turn of defence counsel Aubrey Myserson. He initially pointed out Bindon had been remarkably

Chapter Eleven

candid and honest in describing his cockney background and previous brushes with the law. Myerson insisted they would have to look to the fictional character Raffles to find another example of a man who moved in high society while he belonged to 'the criminal classes'. Myerson insisted the jury should discard the evidence of convicted murderer William Murphy, telling them that the prosecution were 'clinging like limpets' to Murphy's claims.

In his summing-up, Judge Mr Justice Mars-Jones said the prosecution's case was that Bindon 'lied and lied again'. It was alleged 'he had gone back on every reference he made about the other defendants to police'. The jury were also warned not to let their judgement be clouded by prejudice against 'clubs where disorder and violence seem to abide'. Then he added, 'There is ample evidence that John Darke acted in a highly provocative way in sitting astride Bindon who was on his back begging for mercy. Darke was stabbing him and cutting him at will and, were it not for the intervention of Lennie Osborne, Bindon might well have met his death.

'You may think that there is little doubt that he feared his end was nigh, if his evidence is to be accepted. If that is right, it is difficult to imagine a stronger provocation than that to which Bindon was subjected. It is for you to decide whether he may have lost his self-control as a result of it, and whether a reasonable man of his age carrying a knife might well have acted as he did and stabbed Darke to death.'

However, the judge admitted that hints of a cover-up still surrounded the case. There were suggestions that a false story was made up for the police about what happened

BINDON

that night. 'You may have a strong feeling that you have not been told everything that happened.'

On 12 November, the jury was sent out. The fate of John Bindon hung in the balance. They spent more than six hours trying to decide whether he was a murderer before asking the trial judge for guidance on a point of law. Then they went on with their discussions behind closed doors. Mr Justice Mars-Jones told the jury he was prepared to accept a majority verdict of not less than ten to two. Then he sent them away to spend a night in a nearby hotel to consider their verdict.

During that long wait for the jury's decision, Bindon turned at one stage to Vicki Hodge, tapped his chin with the back of his hand and said, 'Keep your pecker up.'

The following day, the jury returned first thing in the morning to announce that John Bindon was not guilty of John Darke's murder. There were cheers from the public gallery. Then came a burst of applause and Bindon smiled up at his fifteen-year-old daughter Kelly in the public gallery. Mr Justice Mars-Jones demanded silence. The jury then also found Bindon not guilty of manslaughter and an affray charge. Vicki Hodge looked overjoyed and mouthed the words 'I love you'. Both his co-defendants Bohm and Galbraith were found guilty of affray charges. They got three- and four-year sentences respectively. The judge told them, 'You two were rightly convicted of making an affray in that club on that night. You were both close friends of the deceased Darke, who was a sinister figure in criminal circles. You both encouraged and supported a vicious and sadistic attack on a man who was being cut and stabbed with a knife.'

Chapter Eleven

But the courtroom drama wasn't over quite yet. As everyone filed out, the mother of defendant Galbraith strode across the lobby and delivered a smart left hook to Vicki Hodge's jaw, then tugged her tousled blonde hair and screamed, 'You vicious cow. You're a mockery to this trial.'

Mary Galbraith then dragged Vicki into the main hall, still clutching her hair, before pushing the model to the marble floor along with a reporter who crashed on top of her. The two women, both sobbing, were then escorted to separate ends of the hallway. Vicki, swathed in furs and wearing an 'I love Biffo' badge, sat crying on a wooden bench with a friend. 'Why did she hit me? It's all over now.'

As Mrs Galbraith was escorted out of the building by a policeman, she said proudly, 'I gave her a back-hander and she slapped my face. It was a spur-of-the-moment thing.' Later, she told reporters outside, 'I've been waiting to do that for a long time. I've watched her attitude all the way through. I don't like that woman.' Yet more scuffles broke out as Mrs Galbraith battled through photographers to a taxi.

Vicki eventually managed to make her way through the vast crowd of waiting journalists and cameramen to where Bindon was. 'Jesus,' he muttered to the waiting press, 'I thought I'd go down for murder. That would have been a travesty of justice. There is a hell of a lot behind this – villains who I'd made enemies of in the past. It's a great relief to be free again – I had faith that the jury would release me because I never deliberately set out to kill anyone.'

Then he made a rare reference to his family and daughter Kelly. 'It's also marvellous to be able to chat to my daughter Kelly, and my family again after all this time. All

197

I want to do now is celebrate. I'll go back to acting one day – but not until I've had a holiday.'

Bindon believed the turning point in his trial came when Bob Hoskins appeared as a character witness. 'When Bob walked into court the jury knew I was OK. And they knew I was not the person the police were making me out to be.'

After his acquittal, the *Daily Mirror* laid on limousines for Bindon, Vicki and their entourage to whisk them away from the Old Bailey. A party was then held at the *Mirror*'s palatial high-rise headquarters in Holborn Circus. Ever the professional, Vicki had ensured that they would be financially rewarded for all the heartache of the previous year by signing a deal with the *Daily Mirror* following Bindon's acquittal.

The first episode of the *Mirror* serialisation focused on 'my gentle giant' John Bindon by Vicki Hodge, and how she had begun introducing him to her upmarket pals. The *Mirror* summed up John's role in life: 'He was the cheeky kid from the backstreets who charmed his way to the peaks of High Society ... and fascinated Princess Margaret. Cockney actor John Bindon revelled in the glittering world of show business. Beautiful women flocked round him, and he had a string of affairs with top actresses and models.'

Bindon's acquittal was also greeted with a sigh of relief by the drama department at Yorkshire TV, where the actor was appearing in an episode of the new Dick Francis thriller series *The Racing Game*. The episode featuring Bindon was called 'Horses for Courses' and featured Bindon as a murderer called Terry Flynn. It had been filmed before he had been charged with the Darke murder, but it was only just due for release and, unlike *Hazell*,

Chapter Eleven

could be aired without delay or fear of any legal problems. There was also talk of Bindon being lined up to star in a money-spinning film of his own life story. Certainly the rumoured new project promised to be quite a yarn: the working-class lad catapulted into show business and high society, whose ambitious exploits then lead him into an underworld murder.

Meanwhile Bindon and Vicki found themselves booked into a luxury suite in the Savoy Hotel, courtesy of the *Daily Mirror*. Terry de Havilland even popped by for a celebration glass of bubbly. 'He was in great form and Vicki, as usual, looked stunning in the shortest skirt imaginable. What a pair!'

Police chief George Mould was bitterly disappointed by Bindon's acquittal, and many years later he revealed how the judge telephoned him shortly after the jury's decision. 'He said to me, "Mr Mould, I want to thank you for bringing this before the court." It was a decent touch, but nothing could make up for Bindon getting off. It was a travesty of justice in my opinion. There were so many grey areas in the Darke murder. Bindon's role may have been overplayed, but you can't get away from what happened that night. A murder was committed and he got away with it. Bindon played brilliantly to the jury and then Bob Hoskins gave him a helping hand. No one seemed to take the trial seriously enough because of all that Vicki Hodge and showbiz stuff. Even the crowd outside afterwards cheered him as if he'd just won the World Cup. It was outrageous when I look back on it.'

Probably the only truly innocent victims were John Darke's common-law wife Susan and his children. As Susan commented after the end of the trial, 'I'm not bothered what happens to Bindon now. It won't bring John back. I only hope he feels some remorse for taking a father away from his children and John away from me. It shattered me.'

She was speaking at the Darke family bungalow in Bexleyheath, Kent. Susan never denied her common-law husband was a villain. But she insisted, 'John wasn't as bad as they made out. He loved his home, he loved his children, he loved animals. He had not been involved in serious crime for several years. He was jailed for robbing a petrol station when he was eighteen and the police never let him live it down. He was on bail when he died but it was for silly things like driving whilst disqualified and a minor fight. To hear people talk you would think it was much worse. We had a very honest relationship. It wasn't a case of me sitting down here and not knowing what he was like. But, as hard as he was in one way, he was soft in another. If he was as violent as they made out, I'd have been a battered wife. We had our rows, but never anything like that. A lot of people were jealous of him. He had a strong physical build and was good looking as well – you would notice him in a crowd.'

Just three weeks before that fatal fight at the Yacht Club, Susan had given birth to their daughter Rebecca. 'There are a lot of questions unanswered during the trial but, as I said, nothing will bring John back. I don't feel any kind of revenge for Bindon. If I met him, I wouldn't want to blow his head off. I just wish he wouldn't make himself out to be some kind of superhero.'

The night after Bindon's acquittal, he went into The Britannia and bought everyone a drink, then turned to

Chapter Eleven

landlady Nora Hayes who had done so much to help his escape on the night of the killing. 'Darlin',' he said, 'when I get my Oscar in Hollywood, you'll be right beside me.'

Then he went off to see his mum and dad at Sullivan Court.

On 14 November, the *Mirror* ran a whole page on Bindon headlined BORN FOR BOVVER, which featured his potted history. The following day they ran exclusive photos of Bindon on the beach with Princess Margaret. He was wearing the 'Enjoy Cocaine' T-shirt. But still he never publicly admitted making love to the princess, and even told one old Fulham pal, 'They'll never get the truth out of me 'cos I know those spooks will be after me again if I start blabbering.'

Within days of the end of the trial, Buckingham Palace retracted their official denials (initially peddled by Nigel Dempster) about Bindon having met Princess Margaret. 'Their attitude was that, so long as Bindon didn't claim anything more, then they'd got away with very successfully avoiding a scandal,' one of Bindon's old girlfriends said many years later. 'But John and Margaret did have a thing going for a while and he was extremely honourable about the whole affair.'

But there was another even more sinister threat looming for John Bindon, thanks to John Darke's many criminal associates. Despite official denials from the dead villain's family and friends, there was an alleged price on his head. Many of the fights and incidents which were to scar Bindon's life following his acquittal were sparked because he was on a semi-permanent war footing, expecting Darke's associates to get him at any time.

Bindon and Vicki Hodge were relieved to get out of Britain and head for California in the middle of the *Mirror*'s serialisation of their life story. 'I just had to get away and get myself fit again after my stab wounds and all those months I'd spent in nick on remand. I know I'm no angel and I have a prison record for things I did years years ago, but that bother at the Old Bailey was a different matter altogether. It nearly did my head in.'

Years later, Vicki even admitted to friends that in some ways she had hoped Bindon would be found guilty because that would have marked the end of their tempestuous relationship. She claimed that by the time of the trial she was on Valium, suffering from anorexia, extremely scared and completely broke. But, despite her mixed feelings, she promptly vowed to friends that she and Bindon would soon be married. 'I thought the time we spent in California after the trial would straighten him out. We met our old pals Ryan O'Neal and Elliott Gould. I thought he would get back in the film world, but he wasn't interested. All John wanted to do was return to London.'

Chapter Twelve

Back in the UK after a six-week break in California, Bindon and Vicki quickly went through all of the £40,000 they'd been paid by the *Mirror* for their story. The couple even travelled to Devon to look at a cottage to buy. 'But it needed so much renovation we couldn't afford it,' Vicki told one reporter at the time. 'So I've put off retiring to the country for a few years. I shall be getting myself and my legs in shape and going back to work.'

At the end of January 1980, Bindon's starring role in TV's *Hazell* (postponed until after the case) was finally shown on the small screen. He told a reporter, 'Given everyone else who had been involved in the show and wanted to see the results of their work, I thought it was a shame it was delayed. But under the circumstances it was probably the right decision to make.' He now genuinely hoped he could widen his horizons in working terms, although he glumly admitted to one friend, 'I suppose now it could be back to the tough-guy roles, but I would like to think it's not. I am not knocking the parts I have played before, but every actor would like to try something different. Don't get me wrong – I don't want to play Hamlet, but I would like to prove I can play something other than the heavy.'

Bindon was uncharacteristically shy about turning his own life story into a film. 'I suppose it would make quite a good film and a couple of people have raised the idea, but it's the last thing I want to do. I haven't ruled it out, though.'

John Bindon may have come out of court a free man, but he wanted to prove to the world that despite his background and all that hard living he had finally shed his criminal past. Here he was, the ill-educated son of a London cabbie who had fought his way from the back streets of Fulham to the forefront of show business, mixing with the top echelons of society – he had even set up home with the daughter of a baronet. But that night in the Ranelagh Yacht Club sparked a crisis in his life, which had turned into one huge contradiction. No wonder many of his old friends saw him as a confused man in the middle of a serious identity crisis.

Naturally, Bindon's reputation as a hard man had been enhanced in some ways by the Yacht Club murder case. And he was certainly a high-profile character now, with his life being profiled in many newspapers and magazines. A classic example was the *Sunday People*. Headlined TOUGHIE CLEARED OF MURDER, and featuring a photo of Bindon in a stocking mask during a TV appearance as a robber, the article began:

Chapter Twelve

> He is built like a brick outhouse – six foot tall and almost as wide!
> Behind the stocking mask there is real menace in his eyes.
> And in his hands he carries a 14lb sledgehammer.
> Big John Bindon, star of TV, cinema and the Old Bailey, is back in business.

The article concentrated on Bindon's new acting role in a BBC play, and claimed that during filming at a south-coast seaport, he 'certainly scared the pants off passers-by'.

> Shoppers gasped when Big John and the rest of the mob burst out of the place they'd raided armed to the teeth with sawn-off shotguns.
> Even a copper on duty specifically to see that no one mistook the raid for the real thing blinked twice when Mr Bindon hammered home a point by demolishing a phone booth.

Bindon claimed he thought long and hard before taking on the controversial role. 'When I read the script I thought it was a bit strong for me after all my problems.' He described his dilemma to an old pal. 'It was such a relief when the trial was over. I wanted to forget all about playing hard men – off and on the screen. But what can I do? I look tough and no one is going to offer me a part as a ballet dancer.'

Bindon still enjoyed acting, and while inside prison awaiting trial he had learned more regional accents and slang and how the criminal fraternity think, talk and act.

He genuinely hoped the public would forget about his past and give him a chance to prove himself. He even insisted he was not the hard man everyone made him out to be. 'I'm not really a heavy type of character and would love to be offered lighter roles – even comedy.'

Then TV producer Michael Wearing picked him for the role of a robber in a new TV drama. Bindon found it tough when the director insisted on him acting 'harder' in front of the cameras. 'I can't do all this killer stuff any more. I'm drained. I gotta start playing softer roles,' he told one friend.

And down the trendy King's Road, times were also changing. Bindon's high-society shoemaking friend Terry de Havilland closed his Chelsea workshop in 1980 after his bank called in a £100,000 overdraft. De Havilland briefly reopened his business and hired Vicki Hodge as his public-relations chief, but that soon fizzled out. High shop rents and raging inflation were transforming the London of the swinging sixties into a less flamboyant environment.

However, further west on the King's Road, Bindon's favourite drinking club the Gasworks was proving a big draw for punters desperate to spot the real-life hard man. The club was run by a flamboyant character from his local past called Jackie Leach, who had furnished it with antiques and a vast banqueting table and covered virtually every inch of the walls with paintings. Bindon had occasionally worked for Leach as an assistant in his antiques business; now he was back in London he needed an income, so he turned to Leach once again. 'Bindon had his uses and he helped me out on and off for years, but he could still be a right fuckin' liability at times,' Leach recalled.

After the murder trial, the Gasworks gained a reputation

Chapter Twelve

as a trendy hangout for Chelsea types as well as notorious local villains, and Bindon's old friend Princess Margaret continued to pop in occasionally. At first he was extremely wary of the princess following that earlier visit by MI5 and all the trial publicity, but she assured him there was nothing to worry about and the two once again began to get on famously – although there were no more secretive trips to Kensington Palace to smoke cannabis and share a bed.

When Bindon's old Hollywood movie-star friend Richard Harris reappeared in Chelsea, he revealed to Bindon that he too had enjoyed sex sessions with Princess Margaret, at a lady-in-waiting's home near Kensington Palace. Harris needed his help in tracing some explicit photos of 'PM' taken at the time of the affair, which had been stolen during a burglary at Harris's home. Harris feared they could fall into the wrong hands and asked Bindon to put the word out in the underworld that he would pay handsomely for their return.

Eventually the photos were handed over by criminals from south London in exchange for £5,000 and immediately destroyed. Harris later told friends that he owed John Bindon big time for helping him sort out his 'little problem'. 'John kept all this to himself because he was still being incredibly discreet about Princess Margaret and felt duty-bound to help Harris trace those photos and get them destroyed,' explained one of Bindon's oldest friends.

But the violent demons that haunted Bindon for much of his life were never far from the surface. Jackie Leach later explained, 'Bindon got pissed up one night and thought this titled geezer was looking down his nose at him, so he grabbed a violin off the wall and smashed it over the bloke's head. Fuckin' idiot. It was one of my most valuable antiques. He was always liable to explode, even after the Darke trial.'

Bindon was also still extremely paranoid about the fallout from the Darke case and suspected that some of his best mates were out to get him. As Joey Pyle explained, 'John thought a lot of us had the needle with him but we wasn't after him. I respected Bindon. He was a laugh and he was still very useful with his fists. He was what we call a sticker. If you was in a row he would stick with you.' Pyle still occasionally bunged Bindon a few bob to work as an enforcer. 'John was very useful if I was giving people a pull. He was good at that sort of work. If someone needed a tug, he was your man.' Pyle paid him handsomely to harbour a notorious French runaway bank robber called Jacques Meserac at the mews house in Belgravia. 'I had this fella over from France who was on the run and John put him up in Chesham Mews for three months. John was staying at Vicki's most of the time so it was no skin off his nose. He was very good like that.'

When Bindon did get any acting work, it tended to be a day here or two days there. 'It was never enough work to pay the bills, let alone his lifestyle,' explained one pal. According to his old acting friend Billy Murray, Bindon sometimes deliberately sabotaged filming in order to earn some lucrative overtime. 'The rushes would go missing. There would be unaccountable delays and it was obvious Bindon was trying to cop some extra money. It was a bit out of order.' By the early 1980s, though, he was once again virtually bankrupt with a modest income mainly from crime and helping out Jackie Leach.

Around this time, journalist Gordon McGill bumped

Chapter Twelve

into Bindon and Vicki outside her home in Bishop's Park. 'Bindon was playing Frisbee in the park and God could he sling it a long way! Then Vicki told me there was a bit of "Bindon-baiting" going on. That was the term she used because people were walking past and making comments while they were in the park. She loved it. There were people pointing him out. He was a face after all, and Vicki still seemed to lap it all up.'

Not long after this, Bindon had a 'problem' with well-known TV comedy star Robin Nedwell in the actor's local The Jolly Brewers, just off Parson's Green in Fulham. Gordon McGill, who lived round the corner, explained, 'They had a clash and Nedwell was too scared to ever go in the pub again afterwards. Bindon was not somebody to cross, even after his trial for John Darke's murder.'

Another time, Bindon was in a boozer in Wimbledon and one of his criminal mates introduced him to hard-drinking Hollywood star Oliver Reed, renowned as something of a hard man himself. 'There was talk of a prize fight but Reed bottled out. They didn't really see eye to eye. I think there was too much rivalry for them ever to be big mates,' explained one old friend.

The spectre of crime and violence was never far away in John Bindon's life. His old adversary Ginger Chowles was on the warpath when he bumped into him in The Man in the Moon pub in the King's Road. Chowles's son Vince explained, 'My dad and Bindon seriously did not like each other. Anyway, my old man says to him, "What about round two. You want some?"' He was referring to ten years earlier when Bindon knocked Chowles down the stairs of The Star. Bindon immediately squared up to Chowles, but this time Chowles got the first punch in and floored him. 'Had I been there I would have then banged a chair over Bindon's head as fast as I could and that might have finished him off,' said Vince. 'But my old man didn't finish him off. He simply walked out of the pub thinking it was job done.'

Bindon scrambled to his feet, rushed out of the pub and knocked Chowles to the floor before giving him 'a right hiding'. 'You live by the sword you die by the sword. My dad wasn't particularly upset about being beaten by Bindon. He was more upset someone nicked his expensive gold watch as he lay there. My old man would have done the same thing to Bindon, believe me. That's what it's like between villains.'

In May 1981, Bindon tried to rid himself of the restrictions of bankruptcy by asking for a discharge at the London Bankruptcy Court. He offered to pay the remains of his debts back at the rate of £10 a week. Bindon explained to reporters afterwards, 'Bankruptcy has really restricted me. It's an impossible burden. You can't have money in your pocket. The limitations are enormous.'

And then the inevitable happened: Vicki Hodge announced to the world that she had split up for good with Bindon. The first he heard about it was when he read it in the newspapers. Vicki informed reporters she had flown to the West Indies alone to get over the shock of the split. Bindon was bemused. He told one hack, 'I saw her off at the airport and she said nothing to me. We've not been having any more rows than usual, but Vicki has been very depressed since her dog vanished three weeks ago.'

Chapter Twelve

Vicki also revealed that she had been ordered by doctors to take a break after a recent spell in hospital with digestive problems and nervous exhaustion. One of her closest friends claimed the couple had split because of the pressures of the Darke case. 'It put Vicki under terrible stress, which has now released itself.'

Bindon seemed philosophical: 'She's reported as saying she'll be back when the rain stops – I hope that's soon. I just hope she has a nice holiday.'

A few days later, Vicki told the *News of the World*, 'John meant everything to me and we've certainly been through enough together, but now I need a break on my own. I've been given doctor's orders to take a holiday to recuperate, and that's exactly what I'm going to do. I never thought after all these years we would go our separate ways, but because of my illness and my business interests we seem to be going in different directions. John and I never had a quiet, cosy relationship. I've bopped a few of the ladies he's lusted after in the past so I know how many women find him attractive – he won't be lonely.'

A few days later, her estranged husband Ian Heath finally got round to finalising the divorce from Vicki. He cited her adultery with Bindon as the main reason for the split. Within weeks, Bindon was rumoured to be seeing old flame Serena Williams once again. All Serena would say to reporters was, 'John has always remained a friend of mine, but there's no more to it than that.'

Three months after the split, and following her return to London from the West Indies, Vicki was savagely beaten up in a street attack. Bindon was the first on her doorstep after she was released from hospital suffering from face, leg, stomach and mouth injuries. She told reporters, 'John has been a tower of strength and proves that love really does run deep. He was furious when he found out what had happened to me. But I have told him I don't want this sorted out with violence. I want the police to handle it.'

Vicki had been attacked as she was out walking with a girlfriend near her flat in Fulham. 'A man leaped out of the bushes. He was the boyfriend of the girl I was about to visit, and I believe he thought I was a man because I was wearing an army-style jacket. He was cursing and ranting and hit me in the face. I fell to the ground and he put the boot in before racing off in a car. I'll make this coward pay for what he did. My face is my fortune, and if I am scarred I will sue him.'

Over at one of Bindon's favourite pubs, The Water Rat on the King's Road, a new kind of girl was appearing on the horizon. They were rich young things with too much time on their hands and a fondness for fixing heroin. One such poor little rich girl was called Jayne Harries, who'd started using drugs in her mid-teens and eventually turned into a lonely, bedraggled, figure often found drinking alone in many of Bindon's favourite pubs.

Jayne had enjoyed her first sniff of cocaine at a party in Chelsea when she was fifteen. As Vicki Hodge later explained, 'She was rich, beautiful, vivacious. She had everything. The whole social structure this kid found herself in drove her to find other misfits. She always latched on to them.' Bindon first spotted Jayne when she was sixteen and tried his hardest to steer her away from the bad influences. She eventually died aged twenty-five after giving herself a fix with a dirty needle in a public lavatory.

Chapter Twelve

Her stepfather later said, 'She made a mess of her life and she knew it.'

Bindon had recently gained a reputation on the manor as a 'good egg' prepared to help sort out people's problems. 'Bindon was now seen as this kind of Robin Hood figure, always happy and willing to help out, even though he had enough problems of his own,' explained one old friend.

Miley Khailani, the daughter of one of Bindon's oldest school friends Barry D'Arcy, had suffered a difficult upbringing, including stays in a number of children's homes. She was in her early teens when Bindon became her knight in shining armour. Miley takes up the story: 'I called him Uncle John because we became closer than most real relatives. I didn't even know he had criminal connections when we first met when I was just a kid. I was one of those typical tearaway kids, always out sniffing glue and getting into trouble. One time, John caught me stinking of glue when I walked into our house and he had a right go at me, and I ran up to my bedroom in tears. Then he came up and sat next to me and tried to explain what I was doing was all wrong. We both ended up crying. "Listen, kid, this is not the right way to go about your life," he said to me. I was about nine or ten at the time, so his words had a real effect on me.'

Miley was living on a notorious housing estate in Hanwell, west London, at the time. Her father was not around and her mother was in a semi-permanent haze of drink and drugs. 'John came down to the house and threw all these druggies out and helped me tidy it up and get it straight.'

On another occasion, Bindon rounded on a bunch of

local kids who were bullying Miley. 'He ended up dangling some bloke by his ankles off a balcony. Then he dropped him on his head and went down the stairs again and dragged him all the way back up the stairs and did it again until he promised to stop attacking me. John was like a dad to me in many ways. He was there as I grew up. He'd often be in my dad's house cooking food, laughing, joking and having a good time.'

He even travelled as far as Wales to visit Miley in a children's home where she was sent in her early teens. Some weekends, Miley was allowed out of the home and stayed at a friend's flat in Fulham. 'John didn't like me staying there and when a man attacked me John went mad; the next time I saw this fella he made him get on his hands and knees and beg me for forgiveness. John warned me to keep away from certain people, and he scared off quite a few of my boyfriends, but he did it all because he was worried about me.'

When Bindon heard from Miley's father that she was on drugs and had gone round to see a local heroin dealer in the King's Road with a girlfriend, he went into action once again. 'John was with this other girl's mum and he's banging on the door. Then it opens and he charges in, kicks the dealer right between the legs and drags me and the other girl down the stairs and into the street. He was so angry with us and we deserved it.'

Another time, Bindon broke into a flat in South Kensington to rescue Miley after two older men had drugged her and then kidnapped her for sex. 'One of them had a gun and it was very scary. But John saved me. I would probably be dead by now if it hadn't been for him.'

Chapter Twelve

Miley's abiding memory is of Bindon putting her over his shoulder and walking out of the apartment, shouting at the two men, 'I'll be back for you later!'

Bindon was gaining a reputation for 'cutting up' a lot of drug dealers in Fulham and Chelsea. And he still continued to carry a knife down the side of his cowboy boots for protection. Miley recalled, 'I'll never forget the time John pulled his knife out to carve the turkey one Christmas. He did all the cooking that day and it was the best Christmas I ever had as a kid. He got the knife sharpener out and started telling all these stories.'

Bindon became close to the upper-class mother and father of a *Vogue* model called Clemmie Simon whom Bindon regularly rescued from drug dens and other dodgy situations. 'He even cooked a lot of food for Clemmie's parents at their house in Battersea – especially when Clemmie went off the rails,' says Miley. Mr and Mrs Simon encouraged Bindon to go to their house in the south of France to help try to wean their beautiful daughter off heroin. 'If Clemmie went on one, her mother would call up John to help try and find her. Then it was either down to their farm in Kent or house in France to get her cleaned up.'

Back at his mum and dad's place in Sullivan Court, life went on. Ciss still cut a glamorous figure in dark fur coats, long peroxide hair and sunglasses; Dennis was still working as a cabbie; and they both assured John that he was always welcome at home any time. 'It was important to John that he could seek sanctuary at his family's home,' explained his old friend John Aitkens. And, when he was skint, he would often pop back to the flats on Peterborough Road, grab himself a sandwich and then nick a tenner from behind the mantelpiece clock before disappearing.

His older brother Michael was suffering his own demons. By the early 1980s, he was often to be found sipping cider on local park benches, although Bindon made sure he was always welcome at the tiny house in Chesham Mews. 'Michael was a very bright bloke,' Miley recalled, 'but the drink got to him later in life. He did spend some time living with a woman in a big house in Kensington. He had a blinding sense of humour, but if you rubbed him up the wrong way he would go mad. He wouldn't hit you or nothing, but he was very good with words. His favourite spot to have a drink was Parsons Green. Used to always be on one particular bench. He lived off benefits and we all looked after him. Michael was always talking about something intellectual. He liked peace and tranquillity, away from all the madness. But he wasn't like a smelly tramp. He didn't stink, he just liked to be on his tod. He didn't want all the drama like the stuff surrounding John, but they were very close.'

Bindon hated anyone hurting his family. One day his brother Michael was sitting outside a pub on the King's Road and a man poured a bucket of paint over his head just because he was Bindon's brother. Bindon went ballistic. 'John later said it was the only time Michael ever asked John for help,' explained Miley. 'John went round to see this geezer and beat the shit out of him.'

The fundamental difference between Bindon and his brother was that, although they were both tall, imposing figures, Michael never used his fists to make a point. Meanwhile, Bindon's role as protector to Miley Khailani

Chapter Twelve

continued unabated. 'One time he came round to our house and this drug dealer turned up. John took a deep breath and then laid him out flat. Then he left the house. The dealer never came back.'

Another time, Bindon turned up to rescue Clemmie Simon from a society party just off the Fulham Road after her parents had once again asked for his help. 'Clemmie was on everything back then. Bindon just knocked on the door, spotted Clemmie, spoke to her for a few seconds and then put her over his shoulder. It was surreal,' explained one partygoer.

This latest phase in Bindon's life can be summed up by his newfound friendship with Adam, a member of one of the sharpest families in Fulham. Adam was eighteen when they met in a local pub called The Adelaide. 'I was a young kid coming up,' he recalled, 'nicking birds, smoking dope and he seemed like a hero to me.' Adam started going to the Gasworks, and one night Bindon and Adam took a beautiful titled woman back to Chesham Mews. 'He stripped off until all he had on was this bowler hat, and then he started singing. It was a crazy evening.'

At the house, Bindon asked his new young friend Adam, 'You want to look at some holiday snaps, son?' He threw over a photo album filled with pathologists' pictures of Johnny Darke on a mortuary slab. 'Look at wound two,' he called.

'Wound two was horrific,' Adam remembered, 'a big hole in his gut where the knife had gone in. It was so bizarre. There was this little weasel of a guy lying on a slab.'

Bindon then had sex with their new titled woman friend

before coming into the lounge and telling Adam, 'It's your fuckin' turn now, son.' Later that night, he dutifully called his mum for a chat before flopping into bed next to his new conquest.

Next day, Adam had Sunday lunch with Bindon. 'He treated me like I'd earned my spurs and, from then on, I was accepted by him. I suppose it was very exciting to be hanging out with this famous character.' Adam says that it was around this time Bindon became much closer to troubled teenager Clemmie. 'He was very soft on Clemmie and I reckon he was falling in love with her. I spent a lot of time with John. I saw him knock people out. I saw all the party tricks with his knob. It was a mad time for me. If he didn't like you, he'd give you a right-hander and there was nothing you could do about it. But John was incredibly well read and had a phenomenal memory. He could recite a page from memory and was the best raconteur I ever met.'

One of Bindon's favourite stories at this time was the demise of John Darke. 'It was hilarious,' explained Adam. 'He'd go through the death scene and how when they'd left Bindon for dead he went for the bowie knife down his cowboy boots.' Bindon would then round things off with: 'So I said to Darkey, "Have some of this, you cunt!" Then I did him and stood over him and heard him rattle. It was a lovely fuckin' noise.'

Bindon admitted to Adam that he did have sex with Princess Margaret, and even called her Ma'am throughout. Then he referred to the 'visit' from the spook squad. 'They put the fear of God into John – no doubt about it.'

Adam recalled that Bindon had a new war cry whenever

Chapter Twelve

trouble was brewing. 'If it looked like something was about to kick off, he'd sing, "Do not forsake me, oh my darling," which was from the movie *High Noon* when Gary Cooper is about to have a fight with the outlaws. It sent the shivers up me whenever I heard Bindon sing it.' The two men spent increasingly large amounts of time at the Gasworks. 'By this time there were aristos, Hooray Henrys and villains all hanging out together in this one place. You could do whatever you wanted and sit there until five in the morning boozing. It was a completely surreal place in many ways. I loved going in there and it had a great atmosphere. I had never been anywhere like it before in my life. There were always interesting people in there.'

What amazed Adam most was the way Bindon stayed fit, even though he rarely went to a gym. 'I know he did a lot of walking because he didn't drive, but he was as fit as a fiddle.' And his mammoth appetite continued to astound his friends and associates. 'Bindon told one joke about how he once sailed across to America on the *Queen Mary* and lost all his money gambling, so he bet a bunch of Chinese chefs that he could eat six steamed rabbits and he did and won a grand. When you went out with Bindon, he was the ultimate consumer. He'd drink a pint of lager, eat and fuck in that order. He was obsessed with it.'

One day Adam got caught up in a sinister Bindon bust-up down at the Gasworks club. 'There was knives and axes and Bindon was standing against the door desperately trying to stop this bunch of hoods from coming in. Then an axe came slicing through the door – literally. Bindon pushed a cupboard against the door and they finally fucked off, but it was terrifying.'

On another occasion, Adam's uncle was in the Gasworks when a gang of villains poured petrol all around the entrance to the club and threatened to set fire to it. Bindon charged outside and they drove off in a hurry. He even lobbed a champagne bottle at their car.

One night Vicki Hodge came out of the ladies lavatory in a Chelsea nightclub and overheard a girl showing off about her 'boyfriend John Bindon'. Vicki said later that the girl in question was young and beautiful. She was devastated and became even more determined to cut Bindon out of her life forever. She put her flat on the market and packed up all her possessions. He turned up a few hours later to find the flat was all packed up. Vicki told him she was leaving. 'You wouldn't dare ...' he said.

Vicki then informed her favourite Fleet Street tabloids she was quitting the UK for good to get away from him. 'John keeps turning up on my doorstep and ringing at all hours to tell me he loves me,' she told the *News of the World*. 'But I'm just not interested in his life any more. He really is in a sorry state. I'll love him until the day I die, but my life would stop functioning if I stayed with him. He's going down and down – but I'm going to make sure I'm on the up and up!'

Vicki had been on the dole since the previous Christmas, but then her old friend – and former love rival – Angie Bowie bought her a ticket for a round-the-world cruise and the pair were about to take off together. She also had a handsome twenty-one-year-old bodybuilder lover called Cliff Elliott to keep her satisfied in bed. 'I'm broke, and times are hard,' she said. 'But I'm not down at heart. I've survived all the ups and downs in my years with John and

Chapter Twelve

my financial problems. John has never been the same since he was cleared of murder at the Old Bailey. He has lost his sparkle, his wit, his sense of humour – his zest for life. Now all his old showbiz and society friends have disappeared. I tried to help him, but I couldn't do it alone. He has had practically no offers of work since the trial, and spends all his time with the sort of people I'd have thought he'd run a mile from. One of the saddest things is that everybody John meets can't resist asking him what it was like to kill a man – so he can never forget his ordeal. But now I'm fed up with the whole business. John's constant calls just upset me. I just want to go out and get my teeth back into life.'

Angie Bowie was staying at Vicki's flat at the time, and Vicki told the *News of the World* she would quit the UK completely after her return from their world cruise. 'My plans for the future may mean America. Angie wants me to do promotional work for her horse stud farm, and I can stay with my sister there and explore a few avenues. There are still a lot of men out there, and maybe there's one for me.'

When the *News of the World* tracked Bindon down to ask him what he thought of Vicki's comments, he replied, 'I have no comment to make.'

Bindon did take a small part as yet another bank robber in a BBC drama, although he had some serious misgivings about taking the role. 'In this business you can't afford to turn down work. My first inclination was to say no. But, unless they're a Brando or a Newman, actors don't turn down jobs.'

In September 1982, Bindon's friendship with teenage model Clemmie Simon was revealed in a tabloid newspaper gossip column. There was even a reference to the fact he was spending a lot of time at her family home in Battersea. But his main priority at this time was to earn some decent wedge. He was paid a tidy sum to work as a minder to a businessman travelling to Israel. The trip went off without incident (for a change!) and he decided he should expand his activities as a minder and even joined a security agency in the hope of getting more work.

But trouble was never far away. Early one morning, a man called John Connolly and his girlfriend crossed Bindon's path in Gloucester Road, Kensington, and 'for no apparent reason' he threatened Connolly who then ran off with Bindon in pursuit. A few minutes later Connolly reappeared and Bindon threw a lump of concrete at him. It missed, but was seen by a passing police officer. Bindon then grabbed Connolly's girlfriend and started threatening her. Bindon's long-suffering lawyer Anthony Block told the court after his arrest that his client had been celebrating his thirty-ninth birthday and was about to call a taxi when Connolly bumped into him. Bindon was fined £100 with £50 costs, and bound over to keep the peace. Magistrate Eric Crowther told Bindon, 'I regret that I have not had the pleasure of seeing you act to my knowledge, except here.'

Many of Bindon's oldest friends believe he had been nursing a broken heart and had gone into emotional freefall ever since the most recent split with Vicki, who had eventually gone to live in Barbados rather than the United States. Within months of arriving on the island, however, she was in the headlines after Prince Andrew sailed in and ended up enjoying a romp with two British

Chapter Twelve

women she knew. Vicki then masterminded the sale of intimate photos of the prince to the British tabloids. Back in London, Bindon and his mates were hardly surprised when they heard she had signed a contract with the *Daily Mirror* for £40,000. Vicki even admitted to one paper, 'I set the whole thing up so I could sell the story and make a bit of money.' She had artfully – and secretly – taken photos of Andrew having 'a kiss and a cuddle' with her friend, twenty-one-year-old Tracie Lamb. Bindon just thanked his lucky stars he had never told Vicki the whole truth about what really happened with Princess Margaret.

In September 1984, he landed himself in yet more trouble when he was arrested for threatening an off-duty policeman. He later claimed he mistook Detective Constable Neville Sprague for a man who had been threatening to kill him and his family since his acquittal for the murder of John Darke. At Knightsbridge Crown Court, prosecutor Richard McGregor-Johnson said that Bindon approached the officer in a Kensington restaurant, held a carving knife on the table and told him, 'Get out or you'll get this.'

Bindon insisted the officer looked like one of the people who were after him. 'There is a little gang of them. I've had threatening phone calls. I am afraid of them,' he told the court. His eventual conviction for having the knife as an offensive weapon was overturned, but a conviction for threatening behaviour was upheld, although a two-month jail sentence was suspended for two years. Outside court, Bindon said, 'Now I won't have to play five-a-side football with George Best!' – a reference to the imprisonment of Best for drink-driving.

Soon afterwards, he was arrested for smashing a restaurant

window in Fulham. Bindon was charged with causing damage worth £10 and remanded on bail by west London magistrates until 1 March so he could take legal advice. He was eventually cleared after the police, on the instructions of the director of public prosecutions, offered no evidence.

Not long afterwards, struggling to find acting work, he agreed to play a naval rating in a play at the King's Head in Islington. Despite the modest £50-a-week role, admirers still swarmed around him after each performance. He told the *Daily Express*'s William Hickey column he was getting too old for crime. 'I just want to concentrate on acting. Everybody knows their lines better than I do. I don't know what I'll do after this play. I've got nothing lined up. I just have to take life day to day.'

But the shadow of Princess Margaret still hung over his life. On 25 September 1986, the *Sun* newspaper carried a story claiming that drugs-squad officers had raided a cocaine dealer's home and found a message from one of Princess Margaret's staff on his answering machine. The story had first emerged at Knightsbridge Crown Court the previous day when a record producer called Tony Eyers admitted conspiracy to supply cocaine. He was fined £2,500 and given a two-year suspended jail sentence. The princess's name was not mentioned in court, but her friend Roddy Llewellyn was friendly with Eyers, who had helped him produce a pop single eight years earlier. Buckingham Palace refused to comment on the allegations.

But one drugs-squad detective told reporters, 'We've all heard rumours but there has been a clampdown on information. Officers have been told not to talk.'

Eyers was reported in the *Sun* to have said, 'I deeply

Chapter Twelve

regret Princess Margaret's name was brought into this, but it was entirely innocent.' Two other men were also prosecuted in the same case, and one of them was known to John Bindon. Years later, one of his oldest friends told this author, 'John paid that geezer a little visit to ensure he didn't try and land Princess Margaret in the shit. John was always very protective towards her.'

Another friend explained, 'John told me the princess snorted cocaine that was bought for her through certain people he was acquainted with. Bindon told the princess to watch her back. I think she was very grateful for his help. He also told her to lay off the hard stuff.'

Bindon still only occasionally got involved with any criminal activities. When his old Fulham pal, professional robber Alan Stanton, asked him to accompany him to 'sort out a few problems' with a fence in Chelsea, he got a terrible shock. 'Alan opened the boot of his car and it was filled with guns and machetes,' explained Mona, Bindon's ex-lover and later Stanton's wife. 'Alan then said, "Right, let's get to work," but John freaked out and said, "No way," to Alan and ran off. Alan said afterwards it was typical of John. He was happy to use his fists but no way would he start using shooters. It just wasn't his style.'

Bindon assured Stanton he was happy to sort out any drug dealers, but he drew the line at hurting innocent people. Stanton put him to the test shortly afterwards when they kidnapped a drug-dealing pimp, put him in their car boot and drove him to Putney Common where they told him to start digging his own grave. The man agreed to give up his criminal ways on the spot.

Bindon remained very close to Stanton, and even told

him that his three recent brushes with the law had been 'sorted out' thanks to his connections with the people who had warned him off talking about Princess Margaret. One of Stanton's oldest friends told this author, 'John said they pulled a few strings to make sure he never got banged up again. He called it payback time. You can draw your own conclusions.'

Shortly after telling Stanton this, Bindon was arrested again, this time for an assault in a pub. He was eventually acquitted. 'But I knew he was telling the truth after that last incident because by rights he should have been banged up. It was obvious someone was pulling a few strings for him,' Stanton later told his friend.

When Bindon heard rumours that Vicki Hodge was trying to sell her memoirs, he seriously considered doing likewise. He saw his life story as the exploits of a cockney charmer who graduated from Brixton and Wandsworth nicks to high-society holidays on Mustique and chumming up with the royals and aristocracy. However, he jokingly told friends he would not be stripping off for a full-frontal shot to illustrate the book. He positively cringed when Vicki Hodge appeared on a TV programme comparing his love-making abilities with her other famous alleged conquest, Prince Andrew. She was asked by an interviewer, 'You've been with Prince Andrew and former tough-guy actor Johnny Bindon. Which do you prefer, Vicki – the top drawer or a bit of rough?'

'I like the whole wardrobe,' she snapped back.

'So,' the TV presenter quipped, 'we're all in with a chance then, folks.'

Chapter Thirteen

Bindon's relationship with posh *Vogue* model Clemmie Simon was encouraged by her parents because they saw him as her protector and a vast improvement on the heroin-fixing aristocrats with whom she spent so much time as a schoolgirl. Clemmie was a stunning-looking girl: five foot ten with pretty, Latin-looking, black curly hair, her face could be a tad gaunt but she had shapely breasts and long legs. As former boyfriend Vince Chowles described her, 'Clemmie always dressed sexy but not tarty or over the top. She had real class and charisma, but she'd also seen a lot of bad things during her young life.' And Clemmie Simon was more than happy to swap chinless-wonder junkies for criminals. 'She loved the fact my old man was a villain. In fact, I think that's part of the reason she wanted to go out with me in the first place. I wasn't one of those druggie losers. I was a normal bloke, very straight in fact. The strange thing about Clemmie was that, although she was into smack, she still dressed more like a Sloane Ranger with cashmere cardigans, twin sets and pearls and Gucci handbags. Mind you, she also sometimes turned up in tiny little denim skirts with cowboy boots on, which always caught everyone's attention.'

Clemmie was certainly no ordinary Sloane Ranger. 'She had no fear of anyone or anything and she had a complete contempt for the law. In short, she was a bundle of trouble,' added Vince Chowles. Her family home across the river in Battersea had a swimming pool and Jacuzzi in the garden, and there were horses down at their farmhouse in Kent. Her father drove a Range Rover and the family shopped in Sloane Square. Once again, John Bindon had got himself involved in a world a million miles from his villainous background.

Vince Chowles has never forgotten the time he encountered Bindon at The Water Rat in the King's Road when he was dating Clemmie. 'He didn't seem that menacing, but he was very loud. Mind you, at that stage The Water Rat was *the* place to be. There were Harley-Davidsons and Rolls-Royces parked outside, and it was the centre of everything in the 1980s King's Road scene. Clemmie was hanging round with a bunch of what I'd call punk toffs, but Bindon was definitely kingpin of the pub at that time.'

Vince Chowles already deeply disliked Bindon because of the enmity between him and his father, Ginger Chowles. 'I suppose that's why I quite liked the idea of dating Clemmie. Just to annoy Bindon. Mind you, I'm not much of a fighter, certainly not in Bindon's league, although I

Chapter Thirteen

did think about running a Samurai sword through him one time.' Vince was treading on dangerous ground because Bindon was by this time officially 'looking after' Clemmie. 'Bindon was besotted by Clemmie and very protective towards her,' he says. Clemmie had already appeared on the front pages of fashion magazines such as *Vogue* and *Harpers & Queen*, but she was spending much of her earnings on heroin. 'I suppose she virtually turned herself into a gangster's moll,' added Vince Chowles. 'At first it was fun having this posh glamour girl on my arm, but then Bindon turned nasty within a week of me sleeping with Clemmie. I've no doubt she told him all about me just to wind him up. She even gave him my phone number.'

One night, Vince got a call from his love rival Bindon. 'It was bizarre,' he recalled. 'He played a pop song down the phone and then came on the line.'

'I'm gonna come round and cut your bollocks off,' Bindon told him. 'You are a dead man.'

'Then he carried on playing this song. I didn't know what the fuck was happening.' The line went silent for a few seconds. 'Suddenly there's a torrent of abuse,' Chowles later recalled.

'You're a cunt. Your old man's a cunt. I'll cut your fuckin' head off. You don't know who I am? You are a dead man. Die, boy. Die.'

Chowles took a deep breath and responded coolly, 'Where are you, John?'

'Why you fuckin' asking me that? Who the fuck d'you think you are?'

So Chowles repeated his question. 'I said, where are you?'

'Fuck off!' screamed Bindon, slamming the phone down.

Chowles later recalled, 'I was frightened and worried. This was the biggest grade-A lunatic in west London and he wanted to kill me because I was bonking a girl he had a soft spot for.'

Three days later, Chowles was wandering down the King's Road when he spotted Bindon right in front of him. 'He was no more than ten paces away from me and looking straight at me. I thought, Oh fuck, this is it. I'm a dead man. I then casually walked across the road and once I was across I turned round expecting him to be right behind me and he's not even recognised me – thank God!'

Chowles then contacted two of his toughest mates who were in the Territorial Army. 'We decided to sort out Bindon once and for all. They came round to my house and we agreed to smoke him out, so I called Clemmie, but she said she didn't know where Bindon was. Surprise, surprise, ten minutes later I get a call from the man himself. Bindon started ranting at me. "You're gonne die. You're dead." I said, "John, shut the fuck up. Where are you?" He said he was in a pub in Earls Court. So I went straight there with my two TA mates and we was tooled up for a battle. But when we got there it turned out he hadn't been there all day. He'd bottled out.'

Not long after this, Clemmie's worried parents offered to fly her and Bindon out to work on a Kibbutz in Israel. 'They were desperate to get Clemmie off the gear and they considered John to be her potential saviour,' explained one of his friends, John Aitkens. In the end, Bindon agreed to go down to the Simons' estate in Kent to try and get her

Chapter Thirteen

away from all the bad influences in west London. He spent a week with her at the farmhouse and, when they got back to London, her parents had rented a new flat for her in Shepherds Bush. They encouraged Bindon to stay with her in the hope he could continue to keep her off heroin. Clemmie's mother told this author in late 2004, 'They were very close and did go out for more than eight years. They really were in love.'

Crazy, uninhibited Clemmie continued to keep Bindon under her spell. Her sexual demands seemed to know no boundaries, according to Vince Chowles. 'She complained about sex all the time. Whatever you did with her, she always wanted to do more. Her great catchphrase was, "We're supposed to be in love and we don't have sex enough and my tits aren't big enough and my arse isn't big enough." The trouble was that once she took drugs she would do anything.'

One day Bindon virtually had to kidnap Clemmie and hold her prisoner at Chesham Mews in yet another bid to get her off heroin. 'It was a heavy scene and John really was her saviour,' said John Aitkens. But there were lighter moments: Bindon often visited Clemmie's parents' home in Battersea and would end up spending the whole evening lounging in their Jacuzzi. 'Her mum took the attitude that John was a good protector for Clemmie and was better for her than the junkies. They wanted him to keep rescuing her.'

But there were more problems on the horizon for John Bindon's life in the second half of the 1980s. Even the simplest jobs often ended in trouble. On 10 February 1987, he was arrested and bailed to appear in court accused of threatening to petrol-bomb a woman's home. He was alleged to have gone to a house in Wandsworth to collect a debt from the owner's husband's father; but, when he discovered the man wasn't at home, he threatened to throw a petrol bomb through the window. Then, in June, a warrant was issued for his arrest after he failed to appear at Marlborough Street Magistrates' Court. He was eventually arrested following a car chase along Edgware Road. After police stopped the vehicle, they claimed they saw Bindon slip a knife under his feet. He said he was only in the car getting a lift from a nightclub in Chelsea to 'see a young lady'.

The original case was eventually dismissed in August when Bindon admitted going to the house in Wandsworth and 'using bad language' but denied any bomb threat. Asked by his counsel if a bomb threat would have forced the man to pay up, Bindon replied, 'It wouldn't have made any difference – he didn't give a damn.'

He was then fortunate to walk free from court on the knife charges after the judge expressed sympathy about the 'precarious' nature of his job as an actor. Judge Christopher Hordern, whose brother was actor Sir Michael Hordern, told him, 'My first reaction was that anyone carrying this knife with him must go to prison.' But having heard that he supposedly had a forthcoming role in the West End play *QR and A1*, he told him, 'I am reluctant to do anything to stop you getting work offered to you.' Bindon was then given a six-month suspended sentence and fined £250 with £300 costs. Yet again he had avoided prison, and he continued to tell a number of close and trusted friends that the spooks had kept him out of

Chapter Thirteen

jail because they didn't want him blabbering about Princess Margaret.

One of Bindon's romantic conquests around this time noticed the so-called hard man had definitely mellowed; but in the pubs of Chelsea and Fulham, his drinking buddies continued to include a bizarre mixture of characters, including Liberal peer's son Matthew Freud, a close friend of Clemmie Simon. John Aitkens explained, 'Freud was this posh little fella, but he had a cheeky side to him and John liked him a lot. He was a charming young fella who seemed genuinely intrigued by us because he came from the other side of the tracks.' On one occasion, Bindon, Freud and Aitkens were stopped by the police while walking along the North End Road. 'The Old Bill were always on John's back. One of them asked which one of us was called John and I said, "I am," which, strictly speaking, was true. The younger cozzer started to pat me down and then looked at my cowboy boots and said, "This must be him." Then they took me to Fulham Police Station. But when I walked in, the desk sergeant said, "Who's this then? Bindon's twice the size of this bloke." I only got out the cells after a call to John's old lawyer mate Tony Block. I'm sure they would have fitted John up if he'd been there. There was no doubt about it. Matthew Freud was very impressed that I took it on the chin for John, and of course John was eternally grateful.'

Some of Bindon's oldest Fulham criminal associates were cashing in on the drug habits of many of the rich and titled junkies who had appeared on the King's Road scene. Heroin addict Lord Bristol was a classic example. 'He was always being taken for a ride by some of the dealers round here,' explained one old Fulham face. 'A lot of the chaps had swapped armed robberies for drug-dealing, and they could spot a mug a mile away and Bristol was a fuckin' idiot along with a lot of those Hooray Henry types.'

Bindon found the King's Road scene very different from the good old days. 'John didn't like all the drug-dealing. It was all about respect in John's eyes. He didn't care if someone came from Kensington or Dagenham just so long as they was solid, trustworthy. But if any of them crossed him, God help 'em!' remembered John Aitkens.

And there were some very heavy criminals from other areas setting up pubs and clubs on the King's Road. The notorious Adams family from north London had taken a share in two or three nightclubs and pubs in the area, and Bindon was paid by one old Fulham face to 'have a chat with them'. The Adams brothers – Patrick, Terry and Tommy – had fingers in all sorts of pies at the time, as well as legitimate pubs and clubs. One of Bindon's oldest friends explained, 'John didn't even know who they were when he went steaming in to sort them out. The Adams went ballistic and John was told he'd be done over if he ever walked into any of their establishments again.'

Bindon had completely underestimated the power and influence of the north-London family. 'It got so heavy that Alan Stanton had to step in and sort it all out. I heard that they wanted to take their revenge and Alan managed to turn things round and save his skin, but it was definitely a close shave for John. Afterwards we all told John that he'd nearly copped it and, you know what, he laughed at us. I don't think he really got it.'

Chapter Thirteen

Bindon then joined forces with his old friend Alan Stanton once again by trying to help him offload some valuable jewellery he was handling on behalf of a major criminal. But it nearly ended in disaster when one of Stanton's contacts grassed them up to the police who then carried out a dawn raid at Chesham Mews. 'Luckily the filth ran straight past John as he was walking towards the house without recognising him, and the raid found nothing,' explained one old friend.

On the other hand, the gentler side to Bindon continued to thrive. One of the few things that hadn't changed was his love of cooking. He adored dropping in at friends' homes and offering to rustle them up some tasty dish or other. 'I think it was the only time when he could completely switch off. John said cooking was almost as enjoyable as sex and I think he meant it,' explained his old friend Mona. And for a short while, he even helped out in a flower shop owned by Alan Stanton in Lavender Hill, Battersea. 'It was quite a sight watching John doing flower arrangements, I can tell you,' recalled Mona.

Throughout this period, Bindon loudly proclaimed his love for Clemmie Simon, despite her problems with heroin. One former girlfriend recalled Bindon proudly showing off photos of the stunning model to anyone who was interested. Sometimes he even carried around her portfolio. 'He loved showing people her latest work,' remembered John Aitkens.

Alan Stanton fiercely hated the young model's heroin habit. 'He detested the whole scene,' recalled Mona. 'And Clemmie's mother kept coming back and begging Alan to get John to try and get Clemmie off the stuff. Both Alan and John adored Clemmie's father. He was a nice, gentle man and both parents were just bewildered as to why their daughter had become a junkie.'

One day, Bindon and Stanton received a heartbreaking phone call from Clemmie's father. She had gone missing after a friend had spotted her entering the home of a notorious Old Etonian heroin dealer called Mad Max in Sloane Square. Less than half an hour later they turned up in Stanton's Rolls-Royce at Mad Max's flat in an expensive mansion block overlooking the square. They slipped past the porter and then tricked the dealer into opening the door before producing a sledgehammer and a machete. Bindon snatched Clemmie while Stanton grabbed hold of Mad Max, who stood shivering with fear as the two hard men talked about what they were going to do to him. 'Shall we chop him up here?' asked Stanton.

'Why not?' replied Bindon.

'Take her down to the car and I'll sort out our friend,' said Stanton, tightening his grip on Mad Max.

After Bindon left the flat with Clemmie, Stanton calmly placed a chain and collar around the heroin dealer's neck and then started swinging his sledgehammer. Suddenly, he changed his mind and led Mad Max out of the front door. Less than three minutes later, Stanton was shutting the lid of his Rolls-Royce boot on him. Clemmie was then dropped off at her family home in Battersea while Bindon and Stanton headed off for a drinking session in the King's Road. En route Stanton – who was on police bail for robbery at the time – signed on at the local police station while Mad Max remained locked in his boot. As Mona explained, 'They forgot all about Max when they then

Chapter Thirteen

went out on the piss. They eventually came back to Alan's flat but continued drinking. It wasn't until much later that evening they remembered they'd forgotten all about Max. So they sent Alan's then wife down to the boot of the car to get him out. She pulled him up the stairs by that collar and chain. Then Alan – being very much a professor and social-worker type – proceeded to lecture Mad Max about the evils of heroin while John stood by as the muscle, naturally. Alan kept repeating to Mad Max, "You mustn't take smack, you mustn't sell it and you mustn't do it ever again." Poor old Max was sitting there virtually shitting himself and nodding his head up and down so much it almost came off its hinges. Then Alan pulls out a bottle of whiskey and they all became friends. And you know what? Max started hanging out with them and used to come to the flower shop to help out sometimes. He was a reformed character and never took or sold heroin again. We all laughed about it later because Mad Max became quite close to them. It was like something out of a gangster film and it tells you a lot about these boys.'

When Alan Stanton married Mona in the mid-1980s, it should have been a happy occasion. But there was an incident the night before the wedding. 'We were all in a pub in World's End,' Mona recalled, 'and this guy walked in and tried to chat me up, which was a very disrespectful thing to do as far as Alan and John were concerned. Alan asked him to leave and explained that I was his wife-to-be. But he was very cocky even when Alan advised him to find out who he and John were before starting any trouble. He didn't take any notice. Anyway, John and Alan came up to me and said, "We're just going outside for a minute." This shows how cold and calculating they could be. They then went to a building site and nicked some tools. Then they returned to the pub and went up to the guy and asked him if he'd found out who they were yet. He stupidly said he couldn't be bothered, and I remember Alan smashing the hammer into this man's head. John then beat the hell out of him with his fists. The man ended up shaking on the ground, quivering.'

But what happened the next morning – just before the wedding ceremony – sums up the rules of engagement. 'Next day, we're at the same pub getting glasses for the wedding party and the same guy comes up to Alan. He's got bandages all over his head but he comes up and shakes both their hands. "I've sorted myself out now. Thanks for your help, boys," was all he said. He was thanking Alan and John for beating him to smithereens.'

And the ceremony itself was only slightly marred when the registrar mentioned honouring and respecting your partner, and Bindon screamed at the top of his voice, 'You gotta be fuckin' joking.'

'I think John was upset at my marriage to Alan,' Mona said later. 'He'd always told me not to marry a villain and I'd made him angry by doing precisely that. I'll never forget when he said to me. "You been window-shopping for villains for quite a while, Mona, but you should always go back to your own kind. Don't marry a villain."' And Alan Stanton remained a career criminal with an incredibly short fuse. 'Alan was always watching his back. Even on airplanes he'd be looking behind him just in case someone was watching him. Alan was a workaholic and he would have made a great straight businessman, but he

Chapter Thirteen

could turn into a really nasty person at the drop of a hat. John always said to me, "Mona, you should be more wary of Alan as he's quite capable of crawling through the window and blowing yer fuckin' head off.'

It wasn't just a few pub drunks who wanted to test whether John Bindon was still the ultimate hard man. Renowned south-London face Freddie Foreman wanted to put him up in a bare-knuckle fight against the notorious Lenny 'The Guv'nor' McLean for a £15,000 fee. But it never happened. Says John Aitkens, 'John could have hurt Lenny, but he turned Foreman down because he thought fifteen grand wasn't enough.'

Foreman genuinely believed Bindon had the ability and raw strength to destroy McLean. 'I'd seen him in a few straighteners and it was quick, strong stuff. Either you can or you can't, if you know what I mean. You've either got it or you haven't and I think Bindon most certainly had it.'

Meanwhile, he remained extremely shy about putting his life story down on paper. John Aitkens recalled, 'I took him to meet this author who offered him a thousand quid there and then with three grand to follow and a percentage share of the book sales. John didn't have enough to buy a drink at the time, but he wouldn't do it. He was still very worried about the Princess Margaret situation and he seemed reluctant to tell the full story of his life.'

Alan Stanton was so worried about Bindon's finances that when he got out of his latest prison sentence he persuaded Mona to allow Bindon to have a share in a wine bar called Punters, which they had opened across the river in Earlsfield. 'Alan told me we had to give John a purpose in life,' she recalled, 'and I said, "What's that?" And he said, "We have to bring him in on the bar." I had a huge row about it, but John came in. It was incredible because Alan was right. John changed overnight and turned up suited and booted and told everyone to behave. He was fantastic. Any drunks were slung out and things went very well to begin with.'

When Alan bizarrely acquired a self-portrait of satanist Alister Crowley, Bindon told his friend that Led Zeppelin member Jimmy Page was a Crowley nut and that he would definitely buy it from them. John Aitkens remembered what happened. 'So we jumped in my Morris 1000 car and strapped this huge great picture to the roof and headed off to Page's mansion in Holland Park. John started banging on Page's front door and caused quite a stir in this quiet millionaires' row of houses. Across the street was an embassy and there were cozzers all tooled up with submachine-guns and stuff. One eventually came up to us and said, "I been watching you for a while. What you up to?" John said, "I'm just trying to get hold of my mate." The cop then said, "What's your friend's name," to which John replied, "Jimmy Page of Led Zeppelin." The copper then checked it out on his radio and it was right. Then the copper said to John, "Mr Page is either out or he doesn't want to let you in because you've been here for half an hour." John said, "Fair enough," but as he was walking away he spat on the door knocker and the cop said, "What are you doing?" And John replied, "I always do that when I come round so he knows I've been here." And you know what? He got away with it!'

Chapter Thirteen

The wine-bar business fell apart after Alan Stanton got nicked again and Bindon and Mona fell out. Stanton ended up getting fourteen years for importing cocaine. Mona argued about the proceeds from the sale of the wine bar and she ended up throwing a bowl of hot soup in Bindon's lap. Stanton even warned her from his prison cell that she was pushing it, although when Bindon went to see him in Maidstone Prison Stanton told him, 'That's my wife. Even when she's wrong, she's right.'

Over in Barbados, Vicki Hodge had been trying for three years to get pregnant with her younger American boyfriend Kenny Goldwasser. It never happened and she was left to wonder what might have been if she had had a baby with Bindon.

The one consistent element in Bindon's life remained his beloved daughter Kelly. In 1988 she had a baby boy, making Bindon a grandfather for the first and only time. Bindon had always made an effort to keep his daughter out of the limelight. He only talked about her to close friends, but made an effort to pop across the river to see her in Elephant and Castle at least once a month. Those who have met Kelly say she looks remarkably like Bindon's mother Ciss.

Bindon seemed to have almost completely given up acting. In 1988, he was offered a part in *1492* by Ridley Scott, but turned it down. 'He said it wasn't enough cash but it meant being in Malta for a month, and by this stage Bindon didn't like being off his manor for that long,' explained one old friend.

He then dated a one-time *Penthouse* pet, but their

relationship was even more tempestuous than with Vicki Hodge. Most of his friends put it down to the fact that she was a tough, northern, working-class girl rather than the type of rich Sloane Ranger Bindon usually seemed attracted to. He still turned up regularly in the Gasworks club, but got immensely upset when he caught one new girlfriend having sex with another woman in the toilets. It was certainly an unusual establishment.

Many of Bindon's friends believe to this day that he was still desperate to revive his fading relationship with Clemmie Simon. One pal told this author, 'John did genuinely love Clemmie and wanted to look after her. He would go round and beat up her dealers, absolutely terrify them. He kept trying to get her off it. It was an intense relationship, but in the end heroin won.' Even after he split with Clemmie, her parents occasionally rang him up begging him to help rescue their daughter yet again. As John Aitkens recalled, 'One time me, John and another guy were out together and went to a mansion block on Prince of Wales Drive in Battersea. We got buzzed upstairs and there were these three hooray types there. John told Clemmie and some bloke she was with to go in the kitchen. He then turned to me and said, "Lock the door," which I did. John knocked them all out one after the other and then shouted at us to come out, but I couldn't get the lock undone so he had to pull the whole door off its hinges. We left that flat looking a right state, but at least those dealers never went near Clemmie again.'

Meanwhile, chaos continued to reign at Chesham Mews. As Aitkens explained, 'There was no lock on the front door and John's brother Mickey was often there as

Chapter Thirteen

much as John. The only thing that stopped the front door flying open was all the junk mail which came through the letterbox. Mickey was allowed to do as he pleased. By this time, John only went there if he had absolutely nowhere else to go.'

Aitkens' description of the house says it all. 'It was just an occasional roof over his head. John never had a bath or shower all the time he lived there. The bedroom didn't have a window. It had two stables underneath. Joan Collins's brother lived next door and he used to rent one of the two garages off John for his Bentley, and that gave him enough money to pay the peppercorn rent and have a bit left over. That was John's regular income. All that cobblers about £10,000 a week from crime was crap. He got a few back-handers, but that was it.'

When Bindon encountered people from that earlier trendy King's Road era, he was reluctant to reignite old friendships. Roxy Music musician John Porter bumped into him at a ball in the Chelsea Arts Club. Bindon smiled at him and simply muttered, 'Catch yer later.'

'That was fifteen years after I'd last seen him,' Porter recalled. 'It was almost as if he'd put all that madness behind him and had gone back to his own people. Certainly he was with a couple of very heavy villains at the time.'

And there were still some memorable incidents along the way. Around this time he was debt-collecting in Mayfair when he went into an office for some money.

'You know who I am?' Bindon asked a man in the office.

'Yeah, Johnny Bindon,' came the reply.

'How much you got on yer?'

'£7,000.'

'I'll take that now and come back tomorrow for another five,' said Bindon before leaving.

It turned out to be the wrong office! Bindon always claimed to pals that he took the money back next day ...

John Bindon's life was increasingly in turmoil. 'John always made a point of saying he was a bad actor and that he was along for the ride,' John Aitkens explained, 'but behind the smile he was deadly serious about being a performer. I remember going to see him in a play at a pub once. He had a lot of dialogue and was genuinely very good, but people's perception of him was all wrong. He was seen as a man who'd got away with murder and that made people very wary of him. I knew then that his acting career was almost over.'

There was a feeling building up that things were starting to go seriously wrong for him. He was in decline. 'Like all actors, John was only really happy when he was working. And if he was happy he was a different person. He didn't drink so much and he didn't knock round with his old crim mates.'

He had always been a fast-moving man, but he was starting to wonder if there was any point to his life any more. John Bindon wasn't exactly a *normal* person. He rarely had a *normal* job in his life, nothing nine to five. Acting, even crime, was glamorous work and when he was off duty he mixed in the sort of circles where he still didn't even have to pay for anything. But on the other hand, he wasn't a hardened professional criminal, either. He never

Chapter Thirteen

stole anything important in his life (apart from a small role in that emerald heist). His kick was more to do with being the toughest character on the block, a street fighter who was extremely useful with his hands. That was what he did for people, and why he was called upon to do certain things within the criminal fraternity. He believed he was above having an ordinary job, but in the late 1980s he took a job in a brewery and learned how to drive. He even passed his test and, by all accounts, turned over a new leaf. 'He was so different,' John Aitkens recalled. 'He stayed completely off the booze and went months at a time without drinking. He just read a lot instead. He was much fitter and seemed happier.'

Aitkens got a clue about Bindon's driving abilities when he once lent Bindon a car. 'He brought the front-window handles back in a plastic bag after pulling them off because he couldn't make them work. That was typical John.' But what he did not realise was that Bindon had managed to pass his driving test fraudulently through a crooked test examiner who happened to be a distant cousin. It seemed that criminal inclinations were never far from the surface when it came to John Bindon's life, even when he was trying to go straight. By the end of the 1980s, the glamorous crowd had deserted him — unlike his old friends the Krays who still wrote fondly to him from their prison cells.

Meanwhile, Vicki Hodge was talking openly about the sensational kiss 'n' tell book she was writing, and even claimed that her friend Prince Andrew was no great shakes: 'If I made a list of my 100 best lovers, he would probably rate about 98.' Vicki's book was entitled *The Facts of Lies*, and she insisted it would include an A–Z of her lovers. 'I've been writing it for four years and I still haven't got all the names down on paper,' she told the *Sunday Mirror* in August 1990. 'There are a lot of men who will be terrified that they're going to get a mention. But others have been begging me to put them in the book.'

Vicki eventually sent two sample chapters of the book to Bindon for his approval, but he refused to sign off on them. 'John didn't trust Vicki by this time, and he just didn't want her blasting his name all over the papers again,' explained John Aitkens. He begged Vicki for the tapes and transcripts that formed the backbone of the book. She capitulated and two weeks later Bindon took a match to his ex-lover's sensational reminiscences and the entire project was shelved. In Barbados, Vicki also had other problems. She was fined $3,500 on a drugs rap after admitting possessing $100-worth of cocaine and $10-worth of cannabis. She had earlier been arrested by plain-clothes cops on the beach and insisted she had been set up.

Around this time, Led Zeppelin tour manager Richard Cole was in a King's Road wine bar when he spotted Bindon walking past with a sports bag clutched tightly in his hand. When Cole stopped him, Bindon flashed the cash contents of the bag at him and said he was doing a delivery for someone. 'He didn't look good, like he'd been out all night, and he seemed in a hurry to get on. That was it. My last sighting of John Bindon.'

Greg Hodal also noticed a change in Bindon. 'I was back in Fulham from the States. I called him and he said, "Let's meet at the Gasworks," so I went up there to see him and

Chapter Thirteen

left a friend of mine in a car waiting outside. But once I got in, I sat down with John and we didn't move for ages. Then I mentioned I had a mate waiting in a car outside and John went out to get him. He scared the guy shitless by asking who he was and then ordering him to get inside. The guy nearly had a heart attack! I could see things had changed for John. Although he put on the usual tough-guy performance, he didn't have the same sparkle in his eyes.'

Towards the end of their meeting, Bindon started talking to Hodal about what it was like to kill Johnny Darke and why he never regretted it. 'It was almost as if he wanted to make the point that he did murder Darke, and that the guy deserved it.'

Bindon was regularly visiting Alan Stanton in Maidstone Prison at the time. One of Stanton's fellow inmates was Freddie Foreman, inside for his part in the £7 million Security Express robbery. 'At visiting time you could change tables and talk to anyone you wanted,' Freddie recalled, 'so I spoke to Bindon about all the birds and his showbiz tales. But, when I asked him why he didn't go back into the film game, he said, "They won't have me, and I can't stand all the people in it, Fred." He said he'd had a lot of arguments. They was frightened of him more than anything, especially since the Darke killing. After Bindon's visits, me and Alan Stanton would walk around the yard and have a chat about the old days. Alan was a very solid little fella.'

But one day after a visit from a haggard-looking Bindon, Stanton told Foreman, 'I don't like the look of John. He looks well rough to me. I think he's got something wrong with him.'

'While we was walking around talking about Bindon being ill,' Foreman remembered, 'I thought back to when he'd started coming to see Stanton and realised he definitely had a point. He'd been visiting Alan all through his bird and he'd started out as a big strapping fella but now he looked all skinny and shrivelled up.'

But within weeks, it was Alan Stanton who was taken sick. He eventually died, and so Foreman never saw Bindon again. 'I never did find out if there was anything wrong with him.'

John Aitkens went round to Chesham Mews when he heard that Alan Stanton had died. 'I was with my two daughters and drove to the bottom of the mews and shouted for John. He sprang up at the front door and remarked on my car which was quite flash. Then we had a few words about how sad it was that Alan had copped it. But he stayed at the door the whole time and seemed to be definitely keeping his distance.'

At Alan Stanton's funeral Bindon was clearly not well, but he agreed to give a speech at the service after a lot of pressure from Mona. The day before the ceremony, he had had to 'warn off' a couple of criminals who were pressing Mona for £20,000 in cash they said Stanton owed them before he died. Bindon wore a blue suit, but looked thin and gaunt at the service. 'I remember holding on to him and I could feel his backbone,' Mona recalled. 'He looked very ill.' But Bindon still managed to make them all laugh with his speech at Stanton's funeral: 'I could have been an amazing actor if it wasn't for Alan Stanton introducing me to alcohol.' Bindon also mentioned one of Stanton's favourite phrases, which was:

Chapter Thirteen

'Never do a burglary in Worthing because they've got too many one-way streets.'

'Everyone cracked up with laughter,' said Mona. 'It was brilliant. It made everyone less tense. John was the best speaker. Alan had asked me before he died to have a party and we did a huge spread. We drank until five in the morning.'

The funeral was the first time Mona had properly talked to Bindon since their major fallout over the wine bar. 'When John first arrived, we just looked at each other and said, "What was that all about?" We hugged each other and there were tears. I had pictures of Alan everywhere. We held hands from that moment on, even in church, everywhere. I often wonder why we fell out. I suppose he didn't like me marrying his best friend.'

Not long after Stanton's funeral, Bindon arrived back at Chesham Mews during a snowstorm to find his alcoholic brother Michael had died in a chair sitting in front of an electric fire. According to many of Bindon's friends, he then put his brother's corpse over his shoulder and took him to The Star behind the house where he leaned him against the bar and said, 'We're havin' a wake.' Then he tried to pour a bottle of Scotch down his brother's throat, shouting, 'It's my brother, and he would have wanted to finish the bottle.' It later emerged that Michael had died of hypothermia in the mews house but, as John Aitkens later explained, 'Finding him there sent John off his rocker.'

Bindon was tortured by the thought that, if he'd been around, his brother might never have died. The day after Michael's death, he turned up at the Gasworks looking like a broken man. Aitkens recalled the scene. 'I remember it was still snowing hard outside and John came in, sat down and started pouring out his heart. He said his brother had died and his body had fallen into the electric fire. He kept saying over and over again that his brother's body had been literally cooked.'

Gasworks owner Jackie Leach jokingly told Bindon, 'I thought you'd go first and then I could have swapped your brother an off-licence for Chesham Mews.' Bindon forced a smile.

Shortly after his brother's funeral, Bindon turned up at John Aitkens' house after trying to see his mum and dad in Sullivan Court. 'He didn't look well and he said he was so weak he couldn't get up the stairs to their flat. He was driving a car for that brewery job at the time, but he was the worst driver in the world. To be frank about it, the big strong John Bindon I once knew was no more. He seemed much paler and thinner.'

The first public news that Bindon was seriously ill came in the short-lived Fleet Street tabloid *Today*, which ran a story in early 1993 claiming he had cancer of the liver, 'according to friends'. Bindon's agent Tony Howard then confirmed it. 'Yes, he has got cancer. We don't know how bad it is, but he is not in hospital and I think he is getting better.'

The paper then talked to Bindon's cousin Perry, who now shared the house in Chesham Mews. 'He has been ill and there are a lot of rumours about how bad he is, but I speak to John every couple of days and he's doing OK.'

Vicki Hodge had a brief reunion with Bindon in London in the early summer of 1993. He was clearly seriously ill, and he begged her to remember the good times. 'I've lived

Chapter One

the life of ten men in my one life. You were the best thing that ever happened to me. I should have married you. I'd marry you now. Then I'd die happy.'

Those were John Bindon's last words to Vicki Hodge. Six weeks later he was dead.

Acknowledgements

This book would not have been possible without the help and invaluable input of the following individuals:

Adam
John Aitkins
Terry Babbidge
Aaron Batterham
Pat Booth
Vince Chowles
Richard Cole
Barry D'Arcy
Roy Dennis
Bob Fifield
Freddie Foreman
Annie Gearie
Dana Gillespie

John Glatt
Annie Glynne
Terry de Havilland
Fred Hayes
Nora Hayes
Greg Hodal
Nancy Howard
Jamie Katuin
Miley Khailani
Linda Lace
Mickey Landrigan
Bobby Mac
Gordon McGill
Peter McGoohan
George Mould
Billy Murray
John Porter
Nosher Powell
Joey Pyle
Shaun Redmayne
Anthony Rufus-Isaacs
Bill Scholes
Clemmie Simon
Mona Stanton
David 'Soulman'
Leslie Spitz
Raymond Taghioff
Gordon Wilson
Tony Wiseman

WRITE NOW!

Five-day courses overlooking Mediterranean in Granada, learning to make real money from full-time writing.

E-Mail author Wensley Clarkson at **kdc13@dial.pipex.com** for 2005/06 course details.